SCATMAN

Also by Jim Haskins

Black Dance in America

Black Music in America

Black Theater in America

Hamp: An Autobiography, *with Lionel Hampton*

SCATMAN

An Authorized Biography of Scatman Crothers

Jim Haskins
with Helen Crothers

WILLIAM MORROW AND COMPANY, INC.
NEW YORK

Excerpts from Robert Greenberger, "Rambling with Scatman Crothers," *Starlog*, December 1983. Reprinted with permission from Starlog Group.

Excerpts from John McDonough, "Norman Granz: JATP Pilot . . . Driving Pablo Home," *Down Beat* magazine, October 1979. Reprinted with permission from *Down Beat*.

Excerpts from Stephen Swain, "The Master of Scat: Zoo Wee Do Boddle Dop Di Yop Do Wop," *Valley Magazine,* June 1979. Reprinted with permission from *Valley Magazine,* World of Communications, Inc.

Excerpts from *Variety* issues of August 21, 1975, and July 31, 1978. Reprinted with permission from Variety Inc.

Excerpts from Rodgers Worthington, "At Last, Scatman Basks in the Glow of His Own Star," *Chicago Tribune,* July 16, 1980, copyright © by Chicago Tribune Company. All rights reserved, used with permission.

It is the policy of William Morrow and Company, Inc., and its imprints and affiliates recognizing the importance of preserving what has been written, to print the books we publish on acid-free paper, and we exert our best efforts to that end.

Library of Congress Cataloging-in-Publication Data

Haskins, Jim, 1941–
    Scatman : an authorized biography of Scatman Crothers / by Jim Haskins with Helen Crothers.
        p.   cm.
    ISBN 0-688-08521-0
    1. Crothers, Scatman.   2. Singers—United States—Biography.
I. Crothers, Helen.   II. Title.
ML420.C94H4   1991
791.43′028′092—dc20
[B]   90-25685
                                                                 CIP

Printed in the United States of America

First Edition

1 2 3 4 5 6 7 8 9 10

BOOK DESIGN BY A. DEMAIO

FOREWORD

I FIRST MET SCATMAN CROTHERS IN 1984 IN LOS ANGELES, where I was interviewing friends and relatives of Nat "King" Cole for a biography I was writing at the time. Joan Halimah Brooks, who was assisting me with the interviews, casually mentioned that she had met Scatman recently and that he might be interested in my helping him write his autobiography.

I agreed to talk with him, if he was available, since I knew that he kept busy doing film and television roles as well as voices for various Saturday morning cartoon shows. Halimah arranged for us to meet for lunch the next day, providing that she and I could get to a studio in the Valley where he was doing a voice mix for a cartoon series.

When he was finished, he came out to the reception room where we were waiting and greeted us with what had to be the biggest and warmest smile I had seen since I had arrived on the

West Coast. I felt immediately at ease with this Hollywood legend, who didn't seem very "Hollywood" at all. Rather, he behaved like an uncle of mine and as if we had known each other a long time. This, I was later to discover, was not an act but the real Scatman, as all who knew and loved him had already learned.

When I asked where he wanted to have lunch, I was surprised to hear him say, "McDonald's. It's only a few blocks down the street and I always go there when I'm out here." When we got there, everyone in the place seemed either to know him or recognize him. Little children immediately knew his voice and his infectious laugh. I was amazed by the genuine warmth and love that emanated from those people.

He ate a fish sandwich and fries, all the while signing autographs. He seemed not to mind; in fact, he clearly enjoyed it.

When we left McDonald's, we decided to drive to L.A. As we drove along the Strip, as it is called, he looked out the window and mused, "I never tire of doing this. I like to remember that when I first came to Hollywood, it was one long road and sparsely populated. Very few people, blacks or whites, had cars, but I did—a white Cadillac. I wish I'd known then that we would be staying as long as we did. I would have bought some land."

That was one of the few regrets he expressed during the times we met. We would go to soul-food restaurants and bars on the Sunset Strip and Wilshire Boulevard, and in between greeting and being greeted by friends and well-wishers he would talk about his long career. Or we would drive around in his big Cadillac, Scatman smoking and extolling the virtues of "weed," which he kept in his sock. We laughed and joked, and as he told me the story of his life he was clearly very pleased with the way he had lived and what he had done. He never bragged, and was always careful to give thanks to the Lord and his wife, Helen, for whatever good fortune had come his way.

I liked him enormously and am deeply saddened that this book, which was to have been Scatman's autobiography, written with my help, was not completed for him to see. Scatman became ill with inoperable cancer in 1985. The last time I saw him, he was in the hospital. Helen had ordered a bed for her placed in his room, and she helped me to understand what he said in a voice muffled by tubes and pain: "Finish the book."

Fortunately, Helen has excellent recall of the events of the nearly half a century she shared with Scatman. Though ailing herself, she consented to long hours of interviews, including some that were conducted in Mexico, where she had not been in years, having refused to go with Scatman after she discovered he had brought along some of his "weed." Helen also had kept a substantial archive of photographs and press clippings. Sharing them, and her memories of Scat, was one more labor of love for the man she cared for so much.

This book is dedicated to the memory of Benjamin Sherman "Scatman" Crothers. I'm sorry we didn't get to do it together, Buddy, but I hope you will be pleased with it just the same.

New York, 1991   *—Jim Haskins*

ACKNOWLEDGMENTS

WE'RE GRATEFUL TO CLORA BRYANT, PETE CHALOS, Donna Daniels, Teddy Edwards, the late Demetrius Ewing, Larry Finley, Harry Frye, Phil Harris, Bob Hope, Victor Livoti, John Wesley Lyda, the late Don Schwartz, Fletcher Smith, Carol Speed, Steve Tisherman, Efrem Zimbalist, Jr., and most of all Helen Crothers for sharing their memories of Scatman Crothers. Thanks also to Joan Halimah Brooks for her help in researching and interviewing and to George H. Hill, Patricia Allen-Browne, the late Jerry Zelinka, Rachel Ray, Karen Pickay, Nancy Sherrill, genealogy librarian at the Vigo County Public Library, Lisa Livoti of the Academy of Television Arts and Sciences, and Katherine Krueger of the National Film Information Service of the Academy of Motion Picture Arts & Sciences for their research efforts. George H. Hill and Don Schwartz's office were most helpful in compiling a list of Scatman's TV and film work, and Elaine Arnold transcribed many taped interviews. A special thank-you to Kathy Benson.

ACKNOWLEDGMENTS

CONTENTS

14 **Contents**

INTRODUCTION

THE GOOD LIFE

HE WAS BEST KNOWN as Louie the Garbageman in the 1970s TV series *Chico and the Man* and for his voice-over work in such television cartoon series as *Hong Kong Phooey* and *The Transformers*. But Scatman Crothers, who was sixty-four years old when he first appeared on *Chico*, had paid many years' worth of dues in Hollywood. He was ubiquitous on television and in films; the number of both in which he appeared would make good trivia questions.

On television, he was the first black actor on a regular series, the local Los Angeles show *Dixie Showboat*. That was back in the late 1940s, when blacks on television were offered only comedy or musical roles. He watched the medium mature and lived to see the time when a black could claim a role that could be played by an actor of any race or ethnicity.

His major film credits date back to 1952, with *Meet Me at the*

Fair, starring Dan Dailey. He sang a stereotypical song titled "I Got the Shiniest Mouth in Town," but in being billed fourth, he was the first black to receive such high billing with whites. In this medium, too, he lived to play dignified roles that were not dependent on his race.

Few people are aware that Scatman never sought fame as an actor and never took an acting lesson in his life. During most of his career, which began in the teens of this century in the speakeasies of Terre Haute, Indiana, and ended in 1986 when ill health forced him to withdraw from the television series *Morning Star/Evening Star,* he was a musician, singer, and songwriter. His nickname suggests his original calling. In 1932 he dubbed himself Scatman because of his habit of scatting song lyrics. He spent thirty-odd years performing as a single and leading bands and small combos, traveling around the country—primarily in the Middle West, but also in the South and on the East Coast. So well did he enjoy performing in supper clubs that he continued to do so into the 1970s, whenever his television and film schedule permitted. Ill in the hospital in 1986, he asked to have his four-string Martin guitar, which he had bought in 1931, brought to him so he could sing with one of his nurses.

As a black man who lived for the better part of the twentieth century, Scatman Crothers experienced the greatest changes in race relations in the history of the United States. He himself did not find it difficult to change with the times. As a youngster in Terre Haute, he had developed a personal philosophy of human relationships that enabled him to travel the world with great dignity even in the most trying conditions. He fell in love with a white woman in 1936 and married her when that was both a courageous and a foolish act. The marriage ended with his death forty-nine years later.

There was no dark side to Scatman Crothers. He attributed his mellowness to his deep religious faith—not the churchgoing kind, although he once studied for the ministry, but the daily-living kind. His philosophy was to live by the Golden Rule and to regard whatever happened as the Lord's will. In the matter of his career, most of which was relatively obscure, he liked to quote the Apostle Paul: "The race isn't given to the swift but to the one who endureth to the end." No one endured more happily, or had a better time living, than Scatman Crothers.

SCATMAN

CHAPTER 1

EARLY YEARS IN "TERRIBLE HUT"

WHEN SCATMAN CROTHERS WAS BORN on May 23, 1910, the tide of lynchings and Jim Crow laws in the South was at its peak, and the National Association for the Advancement of Colored People (NAACP), formed primarily to fight for anti-lynching laws, had been established just the year before. Conditions were not much better in the North. In New York, in the year of Scatman's birth, Jack Johnson's knockout of the "great white hope," Jim Jeffries, led to an anti-black riot that hastened the migration of black New Yorkers northward to Harlem, well above the established city's limits but newly accessible via the elevated subway line.

In the Midwest, things were somewhat different. Perhaps because of its erstwhile history as a frontier and its later central position geographically—its function as a crossroads between East and West—and perhaps also because its black population had never been large, the Midwest was a more welcoming place for blacks than most others in the United States in 1910.

Indiana in particular, despite its proximity to the South and its frequently southern attitudes, was marked by a live-and-let-live attitude that gave some comfort to blacks. Indiana was never a slave state, and during the Civil War, when Kentucky passed a Fugitive Slave Law aimed at preventing its slaves from escaping to army camps in neighboring states, Indiana's regiments consistently violated that law.

More recently, Gary, Indiana, became one of two large cities in the Midwest to elect black mayors in 1967 (Richard Hatcher in Gary, Carl Stokes in Cleveland), and Indiana has a high percentage of adoptions of black babies by white couples.

Scatman Crothers was born in Terre Haute, capital of the Hoosier state, on the cusp of the large black migration from the South that followed the passage of rigid segregation laws there and that by 1950 would swell the black population of many northern and midwestern cities to more than 10 percent.

Terre Haute's black population in 1910 was comparatively small, but larger than in those towns without railroad depots. As a terminal for the C.C.C. and St. Louis railroad company (nicknamed the Big Four), it attracted porters, hostlers to work in the roundhouses where the engines were turned around, and other black railroad workers. This population, in turn, created a need for boardinghouse keepers, barbers, tailors, and the like. According to Demetrius Ewing, whose family moved to Terre Haute around 1919, there were also black doctors and dentists.

Scatman's father, Benjamin Crothers, born in Jonesboro, Arkansas, operated a secondhand-clothing store in Terre Haute. He also did odd jobs for local whites. "He was what you'd call a hustler," Scatman said in 1985. "He kept busy selling secondhand suits. He was a shoe cobbler, too. And then he would clean people's houses, bank their furnaces, and all that stuff. He believed in work and keeping busy; he couldn't stand no slouch.

"They called my father a black Jew, because he was always

hustling, always trying to make a buck. He used to sell those suits for five or six dollars; I think the most he ever got for a suit was about fourteen or fifteen dollars, but of course in those days that was good money. He didn't believe in being idle."

Nor was Fredonia Lewis Crothers idle, what with the responsibility of raising five children. Scatman, born Benjamin Sherman Crothers, was the youngest. His brother, Lewis, was nine years older. His three sisters were Frances, India, and Maria, who was three years older than he.

The family was close. They sang together and attended church together, and Mrs. Crothers in particular created an atmosphere of warmth and love in which a child could thrive. "She was a sweet lady," Scatman remembered. "She was giving, nice, very understanding. My father was on the strict side. He wouldn't have to speak; he'd just look at you and you knew what he meant.

"When I was a kid," Scatman recalled, "I used to go with him to clean up and take care of the rich white folks' furnaces. Then we would go sometimes and clean their houses. Sometimes my older brother, Lewis, would help me."

Scatman seems to have inherited his mother's sweet nature and his father's enterprising spirit, and as the baby of the family, he learned early to enjoy lots of attention.

The Crotherses were not poor, but they were not particularly well off either. As Scatman put it, "I was born in the house. We didn't have no money to pay no hospitals. We didn't have a bathtub—we used to take our baths in a big old number three tub. I can remember oil lamps—we finally got us some electricity. That was long before we had an inside bathroom. We had an outhouse. The Sears and Roebuck catalog was on the floor, because its pages were nice and thin. A lot of people don't know that Roebuck was a black man. I used to hate to go out to the toilet in the wintertime. I liked to work downtown so I could use the white folks' bathrooms."

The Crothers family, however, always had enough to eat. They kept a garden and a few chickens and hogs. John Wesley Lyda, director emeritus of the Afro-American Studies Center at

Indiana State University and a childhood friend of Scatman's, recalls that when he was about eight or nine years old, he carried both the *Terre Haute Post* and the *Indianapolis Recorder*. The Crotherses took one of the newspapers from him.

"When I'd be out collecting on Sunday morning, I always made it a point to stop by Sherman Crothers's house because every Sunday morning they had this good sausage and pancakes and would invite me in to sit down. Mrs. Crothers would say, 'Wesley, why don't you join us for some of this sausage and pancakes,' and I would sit down there and eat with them. She was a kind person, and I liked to talk with her. She made me feel at home."

The Crotherses lived at 922 Gilbert Avenue in an area that was called Baghdad because of its sizable Turkish population.

"There were practically all nationalities," according to Scatman, "Syrians, Turks, Germans, Greeks, Jews. I went to school with the Keikenbaums, the Kibbits, the Bennetts, the Nazarees. When I was a kid, some Turks wanted to take me to the old country with them, but Mama said no."

Thus, from an early age, Scatman was aware of the differences among people and of the caring that could exist in spite of those differences. Far from being threatened by the strange languages he heard around him, he was interested in learning them. And he was never afraid of strangers, but eager to make them like him.

His earliest memories were of performing and of making it pay. "When I was five or six years old, I used to put on shows for the kids in the neighborhood. I would take the sheet off my mother's bed and make a tent, and I used to charge the kids toothpicks and matches to get in. Then, when business got good, I started charging a penny."

"I always had one-man shows. I don't remember my brother and sisters coming out and doing these shows with me. They'd say, 'You're always clowning,' and not pay much attention to me. My parents said I was a natural clown, by which they meant that I was just naturally gifted."

The Crotherses were a musical family. Benjamin Crothers played guitar, as did Sherman ("I'd just comp on it, you know"). Lewis played cornet. Everyone sang. "I was the only one who pursued music professionally," said Scatman. "The rest of the family were religious people." But as a child, young Sherman did not think seriously about entering show business.

"I was just having fun. I used to dance and make up songs— I didn't even know what the words meant. And I'd do magic tricks. I'd take a penny and put it in my left pocket, and I'd say, 'You see this penny?' I'd say, 'I'm going to say the magic word and this penny in my left pocket is going to go in my right pocket. Okay, now I'll say the magic word: Abadabadobe.' And I'd pull the penny out of my right pocket. The toughest part of that trick was getting the penny back into the left pocket. I'd say, 'Abadabadobe,' and I'd take it out of the left pocket and say, 'Here it is.' "

By the time he was seven or eight, Scatman had discovered that he could make more than toothpicks, matches, and pennies by dancing on the street—"White people throwing me nickels and dimes and pennies. The Lord has always gifted me with that type of talent—singing, entertaining, dancing." He was also driving his mother to distraction by drumming with her knives and forks on the back of her coal stove.

"She finally bought me a Boy Scout drum," Scatman recalled, "because I was bending up all her knives and forks. I still remember the guy who broke my drum. His name was Poke. He lived next door, and he came over, and I let him play my drum. He didn't know how to use the drumsticks, and instead of hitting the drum, he punched a hole in it. I never will forget that. The first drum I ever had, and that sucker busted it. He didn't do it intentionally, but that was a heartbreaker for me.

"I told my mother how Poke had busted my drum accidentally, and she said we could have it fixed. So I think we went and got it patched up or something. But it wasn't the same."

At Booker T. Washington School, an all-black combination elementary and junior high school, Scatman's classmates enjoyed his made-up songs and comic antics. "I used to take a rubber

band and put a spitball in it and pop cats upside their head and
then act like I did nothing," Scatman recalled. "But I'd get
caught, and when you got caught, you got whipped. In those
days, they'd whip you in school if you did wrong. They really
whipped you! And then they told your father and mother, and
when you got home, you'd get another whipping. So you'd get
two."

"I had quite a few whippings. My father used to say, 'I hate
to do this, but I have to do it.' I'd have to take off all my clothes,
and he'd take that hickory switch to my backside. At that time, I
used to get angry, but now I'm glad that they whipped me,
because it made a gentleman out of me. You know the Bible says
that if you spare the rod, you ruin the child. You can't tell
modern people that. The Bible says, beat him and he won't die.
I'm here. I didn't die."

In spite of being a cutup at school, Sherman did well.
John Wesley Lyda, four years Sherman's junior, recalls that
Mrs. Eva Bell Porter taught English to the junior high school
students. "The kids were telling Mrs. Porter that Sherman was
cutting up, but Mrs. Porter said, 'Sherman might be cutting
up, but he always does his work and he is a very, very good
student.' "

Scatman managed to maintain good grades without spending much time studying. He entertained every chance he got.
"Do they still have those Friday assemblies in school where they
have a little show?" he asked in 1985. "I'd just sing and dance
and tell a few outrageous jokes."

He was also interested in sports. In grade school, he was a
right halfback on the football team, the catcher on the baseball
team, and specialized in the 220-yard race in track. He also
engaged in less strenuous sports, like shooting marbles with his
older brother, Lewis, often for money.

"That's how I got the nickname I had when I was coming
up," recalled Scatman. "My brother was a heck of a marble
shooter, and I'd always be rooting him on. One time I was saying, 'Come on, Lewis,' and this other guy said, 'Tell your duck-
mouth brother to quit talking so much.' That's how I got the

nickname Duck; from then on, the kids started calling me Duck. My sisters and brother never called me anything but Sherman."

In spite of his penchant for having fun, Scatman was a hustler like his father and serious about both keeping busy and making money. While he would gamble on marble games, and later become an inveterate Numbers player, he also worked for his pocket money. He was earning money by the time he was seven or eight years old, dancing on street corners for the white folks. Later on, he had a shoe-shining business. "I had this little box with rags and polishes, and I'd go around and shine shoes on the street corners. I'd get a nickel. I always kept busy."

By age twelve or thirteen, he was shining shoes for John Chalos, a Greek immigrant who owned John's Hat Cleaning Parlor and Crescent Shoe Shine, a combination shoe-shining, hat-cleaning, and clothes-pressing business at Seventh and Wabash in the center of downtown Terre Haute.

"He was a nice religious man," recalled Scatman. "He spoke Greek, and he liked to teach it to his employees so they could talk to each other without the customers knowing what was being said. I really wanted to learn Greek, because where I lived there were so many different nationalities and languages spoken and I wanted to learn different languages. I'd say, 'How do you say this or that,' and he'd say it and then write it down. I learned 'How are you?' and 'Good morning,' and 'You're a good boss,' and different things."

John Chalos's son, Pete, was a small boy then. By the 1980s, he was mayor of Terre Haute. "I can remember when I was a little kid, I'd go down to the store in the late afternoon and wait for Dad to close up and then walk home with him. We'd be sitting around in the chairs, waiting for people to come in to get their shoes shined or their pants pressed. A lot of them pre-ferred Scatman, because he could play tunes with the brushes and pop that rag on the shoes. That got him an awful lot of tips, more than the rest of us. I remember he was more of a grown man when he was a boy.

"Dad taught him Greek so he could talk to him without customers knowing what they were saying. He was one of the few fellows that ever worked for Dad who learned the Greek other than a couple of words. Scatman learned how to carry on a conversation. Dad always really loved Scatman. He had a lot of fellows working for him down through the years, but he thought that Scatman was about tops, not only as a worker but as a good, fun person to have in the place, good for business. Dad loved him like his own son, you might say."

Scatman would work for John Chalos off and on even after he entered show business.

After being graduated from eighth grade, Scatman entered Wiley High School, where he continued to do well in his studies. John Wesley Lyda recalls happening by Scatman one day as he was shining shoes and asking him how he was doing in high school. "He said, 'Well, Wesley, I'll tell you. I'm doing all right in biology. I'm doing all right in Latin' (he started talking to me in Latin). 'I'm doing all right in history. But I'm not doing very well in that math at all.' "

Lyda's father taught math and science at the high school, and he disagreed. "My father said that Sherman had a brilliant mind. He also used to tell me that Sherman helped him a lot with the kids. My father was a strict disciplinarian, and you know how kids tend to react to that. But Sherman would come along and say or do something that would relieve the tension and that allowed my father to move on with the lesson. He used to say that Sherman really understood what he was trying to do.

"My father was the kind of teacher that if the kids didn't do well during the day, he would make it his business to go to the homes in the evening and sit down with them and go over the lessons with them. He'd tell the kids that if they weren't learning their lessons, they were wasting their parents' money and that if they expected to be anything and really wanted to be considered first-class citizens, they had to achieve. He said that Sherman would always tell them, 'Listen to Mr. Lyda. He is telling you the truth. He is telling you the truth.' "

All blacks who lived south of Locust Street attended Wiley High (those on the north side went to Garfield High). Both the city's high schools were integrated because Terre Haute's black population was not large enough to support its own high school. There were even a few black teachers, among them John Wesley Lyda's father.

When Scatman spoke of his high school experience, he would talk about playing football, but he failed to say that he did not play on the Wiley team. At the time he attended, the school administration did not look kindly on integrated teams—or perhaps none of the black would-be players was good enough for an exception to be made.

Demetrius Ewing attended Wiley High when Scatman was there. In an oral-history interview for the Vigo County Public Library in 1981, Ewing made reference to other times in the school's history when there had been black football players: "There was a lull between the [black] Lafoon brothers and what-have-you; they [the school administration] didn't particularly care for the blacks to play football."

Ewing continued, "So Mr. Hyte (Charlie Hyte was the principal of Booker Washington school) formed an all-black independent team, and he taught us how to play football. We had to go to Indianapolis, Gary, Evansville, Queensboro, and East St. Louis to play [other black teams]. But Mr. Hyte would go into his pocket to pay to take us to these various places."

Ewing also remembered, "When I graduated from high school, they had the senior prom. It was held at Terre Haute House, and they went around me because I was black. And I didn't get to go to the prom." Scatman quit school before his senior year, so he was spared that indignity, although he might well have challenged the system and gone anyway.

While the school administration had its racist rules, the students apparently got along well most of the time. Scatman never mentioned racial troubles at the school, and Demetrius Ewing recalled that there were only minor incidents. Ewing was the first black student monitor at Wiley High. Scatman was yell leader at school pep rallies: "Wiley High! W-I-L-E-Y High,

Wiley, Wiley, Wiley High, yeah team!" he could still yell happily sixty years later.

By the time Scatman entered high school, the influx of blacks from the South had begun to change white attitudes in the Midwest. In East St. Louis, Illinois, where Scatman and his team traveled to play rival black football teams, black migrants from the South had boosted the black population to one third of the city's total, and tensions between the races resulted in a race riot. While there were no race riots in Terre Haute, Indiana, the swelling black population had begun to affect white attitudes. Strict segregation obtained.

Recalled Demetrius Ewing, "Blacks lived either on the north side of town or on the south side. At one time, you'd pick up the newspaper. [It would] say, 'So-and-so was killed in an accident at such-and-such a location.' Why, you knew that was [a] black [person] because of that location."

The town Woolworth's had a counter up near the front where blacks could get food to take out, but there were no seats at that counter as there were at the counter in the back, which was for whites.

Terre Haute House, the local hotel, required black employees and visiting musicians to use the back door and the freight elevator. In the basement of the hotel were separate water fountains for "White" and "Colored."

"All the theaters had separate sections for the blacks," recalled Demetrius Ewing. "After you'd get inside, there was a stairway going up. You couldn't sit on the first floor; you had to go upstairs. As soon as you'd get in—pay your ticket . . . get inside the lobby—then . . . you'd go upstairs."

But while Ewing and the rest of Terre Haute's blacks, including other members of Scatman's own family, bowed to custom and obeyed the rules, Scatman, who had a healthy self-image, decided at an early age not to subscribe to the color consciousness that existed not just in the white community but also in the black.

"I remember when I was a teenager," he recalled in 1985, "there was an organization called the Blue Vein Society, and it was for yellow people [light-skinned Negroes, whom blacks called "high yellow"]. Now that's funny—yellow people having themselves a Blue Vein Society. What's also funny is that now those same yellow people are calling themselves black. I can remember a time when if you called a cat black, he'd be ready to kill you, just as if you called him nigger he'd be ready to kill you.

"Anyway, the people in this Blue Vein Society wouldn't mess around with anybody as dark as me, you had to be yellow. And I know some kids from my hometown who moved away and passed for white—two of them used to teach school in Gary, Indiana, back in the 1930s. I won't call their names, but they were passing and I knew they were black. I give them credit: If they could pass, they should go ahead and pass. There was no way I could pass, and I didn't even try. I used to cuss [those yellow people] out. I'd just say, 'You ain't nothing but a light-complexioned nigger. You ain't no more than me.'

"Then there were the rednecks," said Scatman. There were a lot of rednecks in my hometown. There are rednecks everywhere. There will always be rednecks. I didn't pay them no mind.

"I did what I wanted to do. When I was shining shoes at this place on the corner of Seventh and Wabash, I used to go next door to this white restaurant called Thompson's and sit in there and eat. I think I was the only black dude that went in there, and I'd sit right in the front where they could see me. Sometimes black people I knew would go by there and say, 'Look at old Sherman in there, he's a white folks' nigger.' They didn't have sense enough to know that they could have been in there, too, if they had any guts. My thinking went this way: I'm intelligent, I'm clean. I've got American money. They segregate their own selves.

"I remember my mother asking, 'Sherman, you really did that?' I said, 'Yeah, Mama, I went in there.' She said, 'Did anybody else say anything?' I said, 'No, ain't nobody said nothing to me.'

"I guess the people just liked me. Like the times they'd be

seating the blacks way up in the balcony of the movie theater. I'd
go and sit on the first floor. They weren't going to send me up
to no balcony. I did a lot of things that blacks didn't do in my
hometown."

Pete Chalos recalls that Scatman was "the friendliest kid in
Terre Haute," and Scatman saw nothing wrong in being liked
for being friendly and funny. He wasn't going to be treated like
a second-class citizen when he knew very well he was just as good
as the next man. He wasn't hostile in his determination to buck
the system, just matter-of-fact about his own rights as a human
being. Never small-minded, he understood that the world was
much bigger than Terre Haute, and he was keen to learn all he
could about it.

He especially enjoyed listening to the musicians who came
to town. Terre Haute was close enough to Indianapolis and
Chicago to be on the major vaudeville circuits. According to
Harry Frye, who knew Scatman when he was young and who,
like Scatman, was a musician in his youth, "This was kind of a
Midwest center for music, strange as it seems. Considering the
size of Terre Haute, it wouldn't look like it would be, but there
was quite a number of bands working here. Later on, in the big
band era, we had Fletcher Henderson, Ellington, Basie, all the
big bands came through here to play at a couple of dance places.
It's a good area for music."

In Scatman's formative years, the most popular entertainment styles were a mix of old-time minstrelsy and vaudeville.
Ragtime, developed in the 1890s, had been adopted and popularized by white musicians. Blues was being spread by musicians
out of the Mississippi River towns. Jazz, an outgrowth of both
ragtime and the blues, was in its infancy, spurred in its development by the influx of southern blacks to northern and midwestern towns during and after World War I, as well as by the
Volstead Act of 1919.

Jazz, like ragtime and the blues, was considered a low-life
style of music, and it seemed to fit well in the speakeasies that
mushroomed in the wake of Prohibition. The style that Scatman

would eventually develop would contain elements of all these influences.

Recalled Scatman, "I was doing a lot of entertaining at different spots, and doing a lot of shows for the Elks and the Kiwanis. In a small town like that, everybody knew everybody, and I guess word just got around." The piano player at a roadhouse in the red light district of Terre Haute heard that he could play drums and sing, and one day she approached Scatman's mother about his going to work for her.

"This was when I was going to high school," Scatman recalled in 1986. "Some lady named Cammie—I don't remember her last name—came up to the house and said, 'Mrs. Crothers, would you mind if Sherman worked three or four nights a week for me at the roadhouse?' Mama said, 'Well, I guess it will be all right,' and that's how I got the job.

"So I went to work in what we called the Terrible Hut, a wide-open red light district with gambling and speakeasies and prostitutes. All the big-time Chicago gangsters used to hide out there. I bet you can't name a gangster I haven't entertained. Capone was the biggest tipper. He'd sometimes tip a dollar for something. If you shined Dillinger's shoes for a dime, he'd give you fifty cents and let you keep the change. You never heard of anybody being raped in my hometown because there was always a place to go if you wanted sex. I think they still have a red light district there. It was around Third and Cherry. I don't remember the name of the roadhouse—Luscious Place, or something like that—but it was a place where all the big gangsters went.

"There was a peephole in the door, and as soon as they let someone in, they would frisk him, take his guns off, and put them behind the bar.

"Cammie was the pianist, and I played the drums. I used to sing and get up and dance. We played jazz, blues, Dixieland, and it all came from the church. When I went to church, I would see the sisters and brothers doing the same beat."

"Cammie sure could play that piano! She could play all the

old tunes that the gangsters liked to hear. I remember one was 'Ace in the Hole.'

"I didn't get a salary. Cammie had a big box and a picture of a cat on the box and a sign that said, 'Feed the Kitty.' And those gangsters used to come in there and drop dollars, sometimes even five dollars, into the kitty. At the end of the evening, Cammie would count it out and split it fifty-fifty with me. I was making around twenty-five, thirty dollars a week.

"Can you imagine a young kid making twenty-five, thirty dollars a week in those days? You could get room and board for a dollar-fifty a week. My mother used to send me to the store with a dollar, and I would have to have help carrying home the groceries. I used to go to the grocery store and say, 'Mama wants a nickel worth of pork chops, three cents' worth of potatoes, two cents' worth of sugar, a dozen eggs—I think they were eight or ten cents a dozen. Bread was three cents a loaf.

"So with what I was earning, I could really help out my family. They were church-going people, and they really didn't like me being around all those gangsters. In fact, they regarded what I was doing as working for the Devil, in a sense. But they needed the money I was bringing in, and so they just trusted in the Lord that I wouldn't go astray. Besides, my ability to entertain was a gift, and they knew I had to express it."

Scatman enjoyed entertaining for a living, not to mention the money he was making. "Cammie is the one who really got me started as a professional entertainer," he later said. At the end of the tenth grade, he quit school in order to work more often at the roadhouse. "People ask me if I graduated," Scatman liked to say. "I tell them I 'quituated.' I went to Shoe College, a little higher than Oxford. My temperature was a hundred and five. I was a hunchback without a dame. But seriously, I decided I could help my folks a lot," he explained, "so I started working out there four or five nights a week, and I was making even more money."

While he had enjoyed school and done well in his studies, Scatman could not resist the money he could make entertaining full time. Already, he was a natty dresser and a young man with an eye for the ladies, whom he liked to take out in style. He also had a strong sense of responsibility and gave most of his earnings to his mother.

In the opinion of Scatman's teachers, his quitting school was a tragic mistake. Recalls John Wesley Lyda, "My father used to say that Sherman had a brilliant mind and that he should have stayed in high school and then gone on to college. However, Sherman accomplished far more than a lot of folks who stayed in high school and went on to college.

"I am reminded of the time we were getting a combo together with some of the professors at Indiana State University. One man whose field is jazz has a Ph.D. degree. He thought very highly of Scatman. We were going to do a whole program for Scatman the next time he came to Indiana, and this Ph.D. was saying that if he could, he wanted to get Scatman to do some lectures at Indiana State because Scatman had, a 'Ph.D. in action,' as he put it."

Just sixteen years old when he quit school, Scatman was far more concerned with money and action than with continuing his formal education. He still had no real desire for a career in the entertainment field, but for the time being it was a very satisfying and lucrative profession. Besides, he was also learning a lot about human nature.

"Cammie really knew how to get those tips," Scatman recalled. "Some guy used to come in there—evidently, he was a graduate of Notre Dame. When Cammie saw him coming, we'd play the Notre Dame song, and boy, when he'd hear that, he'd walk up to the piano and put five or ten dollars in the kitty. She knew how to work it. She knew all those guys. I used to sing all those songs. She'd say, 'Okay, now here comes the guy. He sure do like "Ace in the Hole." ' We'd start playing, and he'd go right over and put some money in the kitty."

The roadhouse attracted a pretty rough crowd, but Scatman didn't recall any serious incidents of violence. Bruce, the owner, ordinarily made all patrons give up their guns, which he would then place behind the bar until they were ready to leave. There was one time, however, when a patron managed to get in with his gun, and he just happened to be a man who objected to the fact that Scatman had a white girlfriend.

"Her name was Mary Lou," Scatman said in 1985, "and one night we were at the club and I was playing the drums and she was sitting right there next to me. A guy came into the club and had a few drinks. Then he came up to Mary Lou sitting there beside me and said. 'What's going on here?,'" and starts waving his gun around. I called out, 'Hey, Bruce,' and Bruce came over and knocked the cat down, and I never saw him again. He didn't come back in there anymore. I don't know where he was from. He must have been from Mississippi or somewhere."

That Scatman was dating a white girl in Terre Haute, Indiana, in the middle 1920s is further evidence that he was his own man at a young age. He just didn't pay attention to phony barriers and would date whomever he wanted—even at the risk of life and limb.

After several months working at the roadhouse, Scatman had a change of heart. He had stopped going to church—it was called Israel of God's Church—with the rest of his family after he'd started working at the roadhouse ("I was working for the Devil, you can't serve two masters"). Although he did not feel he was doing "anything wrong spiritually," he began to miss attending church and to feel guilty about not going. One Sunday he did attend, and there he felt the call. He immediately told his parents that he had felt called by the Lord, and they were overjoyed. Then he went to the Reverend Barnett and told him, and the reverend immediately took charge of his religious education.

"He was the one who taught me to minister," said Scatman. "I started out preaching to the children, the Christian Endeavor. Later, after I had got more training, I was going to be a preacher. That's what I was going to be, and that's what my mother and dad wanted me to do. But the Devil . . . I let the Devil come in."

The teenaged Scatman had no trouble obeying the Commandments of the Lord, save one: He liked girls, and couldn't seem to control himself when he was around them. "I committed fornication," Scatman admitted. "I was supposed to preach to the children one time, and I told the pastor I couldn't. When he asked why, I told him it was because I had committed fornication. He said, basically, that it was nice for me to be honest but that I had to leave the church."

Scatman was matter-of-fact about his fall from grace. "I couldn't be no hypocrite and get up in front of those kids and preach and done done some wrong. That's why a lot of those preachers on television aren't but a bunch of hypocrites—'Don't do as I do, do as I say do.' That's not right. A minister is supposed to set the example for members of his church. I couldn't be a hypocrite. But I definitely had the calling, and I would have been a good preacher if I hadn't let the Devil in."

In his later years, Scatman would often comment, "If I'd known then what I know now . . ." but he was not one to express, or feel, regret about the past. Still, he would sometimes get wistful when talking about the time he responded to "the call." It was a time of great contentment for him, and even though he fell from grace, the lessons he learned from going to church with his family and studying for the ministry stayed with him, forming his character and informing his attitudes and behavior.

"I'm still ministering, but in a different way," he'd say. "The Bible is the book I read. It's got answers for everything. I practice the Golden Rule. I want to go to bed with a clear conscience. I've helped a lot of people, and I've always tried to help them while they are alive, not just go to their funeral after they're dead."

After his brief stint as a teenage preacher, Scatman, having let the Devil in, went back to doing "the Devil's work" in the red light district. He performed in various bootlegging places, playing drums or the ukulele, singing, and dancing. One club he remembered was called Fort Heyden. "I remember another club I played in. I got real drunk one night while I was entertaining, and they threw me out. But that's all right. They called me back after I sobered up to do another job."

When he couldn't get roadhouse work, Scatman was always welcome over at John Chalos's place, and he often stopped in there either to visit or to pick up some pocket money shining shoes.

When he was about eighteen, Scatman decided it would soon be time for him to leave home and explore the big world outside Terre Haute. He did not want to remain in his hometown as his siblings had done. His older brother, Lewis, had gone into the shoe-cobbling business. He also worked in the local coal mine. Scatman knew there was more to life than that. He set about preparing himself for the larger world by working in a variety of jobs.

"I wanted to do some of everything. I said to myself, 'I'm going to leave home, so I'm going to take the hardest job you can do,' and that was working in a foundry. I worked in the American Car Foundry about three or four weeks. My first job was firing the cubelo, putting the iron in the cubelo to melt. Then I got promoted down to the floor cutting sand for the molders with a shovel.

"I worked in a bottle factory where they made Coca-Cola bottles. It was the Root glass factory, and I worked taking those hot Coca-Cola bottles off the rack and putting them in boxes.

"Another job I had was washing dishes at this hotel from seven in the evening until seven the next morning. In those days, they had those big number three washtubs—none of this automation. You washed in one and rinsed in the other.

"Then I did porter work at the Terre Haute House, mopping with those big thirty-two-pound mops. Yeah, I used to mop those big lobbies. I did practically all kinds of work, because I knew I was going to leave home and I wanted to know how to do most any kind of work. John had already taught me how to talk Greek, and I could clean and block hats. I could shine shoes, I could press clothes."

After about two years, he decided he was ready for the outside world. "I wasn't thinking about no career. I was just thinking about how I'd been home long enough and how it was time to leave home and get out in the world and meet different people and see different things and do different work. I used to sing this song: 'I'm a traveling man. I traveled miles around. I never got tired of traveling till the police shot me down.'

"Before I left, my father said, 'Son, I know you're gonna have trouble, but don't let nothin' hurt you but a lick.' He said, 'Talk is cheap. Money buys *food*!' That's what I've always believed. Words don't mean nothing!"

CHAPTER 2

S. CROTHERS, ENTERTAINER AND DIRECTOR

WHEN SCATMAN LEFT Terre Haute, he had just turned nineteen and had no idea that the outside world for which he had prepared himself as best he knew how was about to undergo major upheaval. In a few months, the stock market would crash, and even a jack-of-all-trades like Scatman would be hard-pressed to find a job. But Scatman thought he was ready. He could work. He could entertain. He could make people like him. He thought he would do just fine.

"I left home in 1929 and went to Indianapolis, which was only seventy-two miles away," Scatman recalled in 1985. "Me and my ukulele and a friend named Earl Gustin. We bought an old rattletrap car to travel in, but it broke down, so we just left the sucker. We hoboed to Indianapolis on a freight train.

"Earl had some relatives there, and we stayed with them. I couldn't get a job in no nightclub or nothing, so I got a job in

41

Kenyon's Packing Plant, pulling those cowhides out of the ice. I used to be so funky I had to walk home; I couldn't ride the streetcars.

"Finally, I got me a job working for Frank Pappas at First Class Hat Cleaner. After they found out that I could talk some Greek and could press clothes and block hats, they gave me a job.

"I guess I stayed in Indianapolis about four or five months. Then I went to Chicago. Earl stayed in Indianapolis. In Chicago, I walked from Forty-third Street down into the Loop looking for work. I was determined to get a job. It was the Depression—the stock market had just crashed—but I got me a job. That's why I can't understand some of these people nowadays who don't want to work. They think the world owes them something. Everything I got, I worked for; nobody gave me nothing."

While Scatman was making a living at the jobs he held, he missed entertaining, and since he knew he could get jobs as an entertainer in Terre Haute, he returned home in 1930.

Back home, Scatman went to work at John Chalos's shop, and also bused dishes at a local restaurant. Many nights, he entertained at speakeasies in the red light district. Through this work, he came in contact with Montague's Kentucky Serenaders, a black band that had originated in Lexington, Kentucky, but had made Terre Haute its headquarters. "I just happened to stop by one day when they were rehearsing, and I said, 'Montague, why don't you let me direct the band?' He said, 'Okay, Sherman.' So I became 'S. Crothers, Entertainer and Director.' I sang, but I also acted as the emcee."

Not long after Scatman joined the band, the group went on a southern tour through Kentucky, Tennessee, Alabama, Georgia, Texas, and Louisiana. They traveled in an old Rio bus—two trumpeters, a trombonist, three saxophone players, four players of rhythm instruments, and Scatman.

They performed primarily for whites at dances and theaters. Scatman remembered the band personnel were paid about three dollars a night. Once, they engaged in a battle of the bands with the Tennesseans and made five dollars. "That was a big night," he said, "but in those days you could get room and board for a week for one or two dollars."

"I had never been South in my life," he recalled. "That was the first time I'd ever seen cotton. We were coming out of Memphis on our way to Little Rock. It was early in the morning, and Montague was driving. I always sat up front with him. All the guys were asleep. I said, 'Mont, I didn't know it snowed down here.' He laughed and said, 'Sherm, that's not snow, that's cotton.' I had him stop for a minute so I could go out and pick some of it."

A black group traveling in the South in those days often faced difficult conditions, and Montague's Kentucky Serenaders had it worse than most because of its rickety bus, which broke down frequently. There were few black hotels, and when they could not sleep on the bus, they had to try to find black boardinghouses or private homes whose owners would rent out rooms. This wasn't always easy.

"Especially down South, they used to think that musicians and entertainers were terrible people," Scatman recalled. "I can remember this old lady dipping snuff and talking about how she'd seen a musician go in and blank some woman's daughter and now he was gone. She said, 'They ain't no good, I'm telling you, musicians ain't no good.' Well, some of them were pretty trifling and wrong, but most of them were nice people."

They had to find black restaurants or go hungry. "I remember when we were in Texas," said Scatman, "I found out that you could really survive off peanuts and water. They had some good peanuts in Texas. I ate many a bag of peanuts. Wasn't but a nickel a bag for a big bag of peanuts. One time in Austin, we hadn't had anything to eat for maybe a day, and the bus had broken down again. The other fellas were in the garage, and I said to Eddie Brown, the piano player, 'Look, Brown, let's get outta here and see if we can find something to eat.'

"We were walking down the street, and we saw this black lady walking down the street with this basket. I said to her, 'Miss lady, do you know where we can get something to eat? We're musicians, and our bus is broke down and in the garage.' She said, 'Well, ain't that a coincidence. I'm just getting ready to bring my sick friend some food.'

"She had black-eye peas and collard greens and yams and hot corn bread, and we sat right there on the curb and ate. It sure was good. And the lady stood there waiting for us to finish so she could take her basket back home and go and get some more food and take it to the sick people. I told Brown, 'Now, let's not go back there with these toothpicks in our mouths.' Those other cats were hungry."

In addition to the discomforts of segregation, there was the ever-present danger of white violence. "One day three or four of us were walking downtown in Vicksburg, Mississippi, and a white policeman was beating up some black dude across the street. We kind of stopped and were looking, and the policeman said, 'You niggers go on before we give you some.' We moved on.

"The South was a funny place. They had these signs, you know, like 'Read and run, Nigger. If you can't read, run anyhow.' 'Don't let the sun go down on you.' And those other signs—'White Fountain,' 'Colored Fountain,' 'White Toilet,' 'Colored Toilet.' I remember when we were in Shreveport, Louisiana, working at the Shreveport Hotel, which was a lily-white place. There was a radio broadcast every night from the hotel, and the announcer would say, 'Yes, sir, we got a red-hot nigger band here. Montague's Kentucky Serenaders. A red-hot nigger director.' That's the way they talked. In those days, I used to hear them say that a black woman and a white man ran the South. I used to go with a girl in Longview, Texas, and had to slip around to meet her because she was going with a white detective."

It was in Dallas, Texas, that Scatman first met Louis Armstrong. He remembered being impressed that Louis didn't use a megaphone. "I'm talking about the early days," said Scatman. "We didn't have no sound system. We used to sing out of megaphones. Yeah, megaphones. Some had little ones, some had big ones. But Louis Armstrong never did use one. All Louis did was stand in front of his band with his horn and sing."

Also while the band was in Texas, T-Bone Walker joined the group. "Our piano player quit, and Montague hired him as the replacement," Scatman recalled. "He could read the cards on the banjo. We brought him out of Texas, and of course he went on to become real famous."

Walker, whose given name was Aaron, was born in Texas. Although he was an accomplished pianist, his favorite instrument was the guitar, which he had learned from Blind Lemon Jefferson, a legendary blues-guitar player also from Texas. Walker, in fact, had led Jefferson around the streets of Dallas for a time during the 1920s. By 1935, Walker was playing an electric guitar, and by the early 1940s he had fully developed the single-string lead style that would make him famous. He pioneered the electric blues that later came to be called city blues and also originated the exciting dance style of performing (playing the guitar behind his back and lying down). Some of the blues phrasing that Scatman developed may have been influenced by Walker.

In 1931, following the southern tour and about a year and a half with Montague's Kentucky Serenaders, Scatman decided to go off on his own. He bought a four-string Martin tenor guitar in a local pawnshop in Terre Haute and returned to the Luscious Place roadhouse for a time before he got the urge to travel again.

This time he went to Dayton, Ohio. Arriving in the strange city, he went to a policeman and asked to be directed to the nearest radio station. The officer obliged, and sent him to station WFMK, which later became WING.

"So I get off the elevator and I tell the receptionist I would like to see the program director. I'm thinking that a man is going to walk out, but out walks this beautiful lady, Barbara Runyon. I say, 'I'm Sherman Crothers, and I'd like to take a audition.' So they set it up. I was playing, and I could see them in the booth enjoying it. After about ten or fifteen minutes, they came in there and said, 'Great, we'll give you five days a week, Monday through Friday, fifteen minutes a day. But what are we going to call you?' And out of the clear blue sky I said, 'Call me Scat Man,' and they laughed. They asked, 'Why?' I said, 'Because I do quite a bit of scatting, what I call flirting with the melody,' and I

launched into a number—do, shabadebadebo, shabadebedebe-
bo, dobedebedebam! That's how I assumed that name. I was on
that station for about six months."

Also known later as bop singing, scatting was an old way of
entertaining in New Orleans that had been popularized by Louis
Armstrong back in 1926 when, in the process of recording "Hee-
bie Jeebies," he had accidentally dropped his sheet music and
scatted the lyrics rather than stop the session. From then on,
Armstrong had occasionally scatted, as had other singers, especially those with instruments for voices.

Scatman had been influenced by Armstrong, but he remembered scatting at the age of fourteen when he was singing in the
church choir and forgot the words to the song. So he made up
his own words, all the while keeping time. "I fell into scatting
because it inspires me musically," he explained years later. "I
like the way it sounds—it's plain exciting. Man, it's my trademark. Besides, this way, I don't have to remember the words."
He enjoyed not just the variety of improvisation one could do
with the voice but also the effect of scat singing on audiences. It
was another way to make them laugh, and he was always looking
for ways to entertain. "Dee-onk, de-onk, de-onk. Jabba-dee-doo-
reep!"

By the middle 1940s, with the introduction of bebop by
Dizzy Gillespie and Charlie Parker, scat singing would reach its
height of popularity as a way to vocalize jazz.

Scatman, who later adopted the one-word nickname, was
billed as "Scat Man, the man with a thousand tunes" because he
had about that many in his repertoire, most of them composed
himself. He was the only black on WFMK, but not the only black
on radio in Dayton. Station WHIO had a black entertainer who
played the piano and sang.

Scatman had a good time in Dayton. In addition to his week-
night radio show, he made extra money by playing weekends at
a local black theater called the Classic. "I did two shows—one on
Saturday night and one on Sunday afternoon. I think they were
paying me about fifty dollars per week, which was good money.
For twenty cents, you could get a whole meal. I was doing all

right. I also hit the Numbers two or three times while I was there."

He bought himself a two-door 1927 Model-T. That was really his only extravagance except for clothes and gambling. "Never was much of a drinker," he explained in 1985, "just a little near beer then with a shot of alky in it. I was always TCB— Taking Care of Business."

By the time he returned to Terre Haute the second time, when he was twenty-two, Scatman was something of a celebrity around the town of about forty thousand people.

"Everybody was glad for him," Demetrius Ewing recalled. At the time, Ewing himself was trying to make money playing the saxophone. "Nobody was jealous. Everyone liked Scat. In fact, I never met anyone who didn't like him. If there is anyone that doesn't like him, no one knows about it."

Scatman now had opportunities to appear on the one local radio station, WBOW, and in fact had his own show on that station for a while. Recalled Scatman in 1986, "I used to call the station W Bow."

Pete Chalos remembers, "Scatman was real popular on some of the radio shows here. My memories of him are that he not only sang and played but also told jokes. He was probably as good a comedian as you could have asked for—had a great sense of humor. One of the shows he put on was in the window of one of the downtown furniture stores. He sat on a high stool, playing and singing, and there would be a live broadcast from the store window. We'd get a big crowd of kids and adults to stand around and watch Scatman be live on radio. That was a big thing in those days.

"He sometimes came to Dad's shop to get his shoes shined. He'd be all dressed up, working in a band somewhere, and we'd kid him about being all slicked up. I think one time he had a pair of pretty near yellow leather shoes on and a kind of a zoot suit. He'd entertain us, and he always had the biggest smile on his face and always a good word for people. He was a lot of fun.

"The streetcars all stopped in front of our place at that time, and people would look in the window and see him in our place, and pretty soon there would be a crowd. Scatman always had time for everybody."

John Wesley Lyda remembered, "There was one routine he did at a dance I went to, making fun of the ministers. There were some ministers who were not as interested in saving our souls as they were in lining their pockets with our money. Scat took on the ministers in that routine. He did this mock sermon and got all the folks stirred up. Then he said, 'Ladies and gentlemen, now let's just pass the plate.' "

Scatman's reputation as an entertainer led to a job with drummer Bud Cromwell and his orchestra. Cromwell and his sidemen were white, and Scatman's professional relationship with the band was unique in those days when integrated bands were practically unheard of. Not until the middle 1930s was the color barrier broken in big bands when Benny Goodman first hired pianist Teddy Wilson and then vibraphonist Lionel Hampton. Even so, Wilson and Hampton did not play with the regular band but only separately in the Goodman Quartet, with Goodman on clarinet and Gene Krupa on drums. Even though Scatman did not perform with the band but appeared separately and made announcements, it was still unusual.

Scatman thought all that segregation stuff was nonsense anyway. He needed work, and Cromwell's group decided they needed him. "They said, 'Sherman, we want you to be the entertainer and director; we've got some dates,' and I said okay. We played mostly colleges on weekends.

"I also hooked up with Sulky Davis around that time. He was the piano player at the old roadhouse where I got my start. I played banjo and sang. He was a hell of a piano player. Later on, he arranged for Jimmie Lunceford and wrote for Dinah Washington. We worked this club for quite a while and made a lot of money."

Next, Scatman organized a trio, with himself on drums and guitar, Leander (called Lee) Barnes on piano, and Demetrius Ewing on saxophone. He called the group Scat Man and His Cats. "We played the popular tunes of the day," Ewing recalled, "but we also played songs that Scatman made up. He was a good drummer, had a real gift. He couldn't read music—he played by ear—so he would just play the song for us and we'd pick it up. We'd all taught ourselves and could all play by ear.

"We played roadhouses mostly—some of them were way out in the woods. We were at Cammie's place a lot. Sometimes we'd play two places in one night. We always played either for blacks or whites, never to mixed crowds. It was mostly for whites. There weren't that many black places. There was a [social] club called the Joysters that had a dance about once a year.

"We didn't have any trouble being a black band. Scatman had a kind of intuition about what places we shouldn't work at. He could meet people and in five minutes size them up.

"He was very popular with the young ladies. It was fun being in his group. I guess I stayed with him about a year and a half."

After the trio split up, Scatman went out as a single again. He performed at Red Turner's nightclub in Terre Haute as well as at the Showboat. Among the straight songs he sang at the time was "East of the Sun and West of the Moon." But his act always included comic songs, too:

"Neckbones and black-eyed peas will knock you to your knees."

"Cornbread and sauerkraut will make your belly stick out."

Most people have trouble remembering what they did last week. Scatman Crothers remembered his early years as a traveling entertainer as if they were yesterday, and yet, in the middle 1980s, he was talking about a full half-century earlier:

"In 1933, I worked at a couple of ofay joints in Centralia, Illinois. I sang and played guitar. I met a lot of nice fellows there. The Leek brothers were twins who were very talented musicians. Doc Leek was a piano player—boy, could he play, and boy, could he drink! As soon as I left, they struck oil in Centralia—it became a boomtown right after I left.

"In the latter part of 1933, I joined up with Eddie Brown and His Tennesseans. Eddie Brown had been the piano player in Montague's Kentucky Serenaders. He left Montague and went to Nashville and organized this band. A lot of his musicians were from Fisk University. He sent for me, and I went down there to be his entertainer and director. That's where I first met Satchel Paige, the great black pitcher, in Nashville in 1934. That's also where I first met Jimmie Lunceford, in late 1933—early 1934."

Lunceford was the most academically trained and one of the classiest black bandleaders. He'd earned his B.A. in music at Fisk and done graduate work there and at New York's City College. He had then taken a job teaching music at Manassa High School in Memphis and organized his first band with students in his class. When they graduated and went on to Fisk, Lunceford went with them, taking a position as an assistant professor of music. The band played frequently in the South, and not long after Scatman met Lunceford, the students graduated and Lunceford took them to New York. They played at the famed Cotton Club in Harlem in the spring of 1934 and launched a career as a big band.

"Eddie Brown was a good arranger," according to Scatman, "and the band did very well. I bought me a 1934 roadster when I was down there. We played some nice spots. We played Cincinnati—Duffy's Tavern out on Walnut Hill, the elite district for blacks. It was run by a Jewish fellow. We used to pack them in there.

"After a while, I went back out as a single again. I played Cincinnati, and this friend of mine from home was with me, and we were driving along in my Pontiac convertible with a rumble seat. We were on our way to Springfield, Illinois, and we stopped in St. Louis to get something to eat. We got out of the car. We both had on zoot suits—with the long coats and the big trousers and the big hats to go with them. I still got one of my zoot suits. Anyway, a guy saw us and said, 'I see you're from Ohio. If I were you fellows, I would leave those hats in your car, because the police are beating up black dudes with big hats on.'

"White cops sometimes had some strange ideas in those days. I can't understand why they were down on zoot suits. I don't know if maybe the blacks who wore those hats were unruly, or what, but I sure took my hat off when the cat said, 'Don't you wear them big hats.' I put mine in the car and went and ate.

"In Springfield, I saw a sign that said Moonlight Gardens, so we stopped. I went inside and asked to see the manager, and when he came out, I said, 'I'm Scatman Crothers, and I just got in from Ohio, and I'd like to take an audition.' He said okay, and I auditioned. He said he'd call me.

"After that, I went to find a place to stay. I checked into the Wabash Hotel, where no black had ever stayed, but they didn't give me any trouble.

"About three or four days later, the owner of the Moonlight Gardens called me and offered me a job. I was the first black who ever worked at that club. No black patrons ever went there.

"One of the acts I was doing at the time was a pantomime of shooting dice. There would be just me with the spotlight on me, doing this pantomime. The climax of the act was when I got all my money down on the floor and I rolled the dice—the drummer would do a drumroll for me—and then I'd lose the whole pile. The owner of the club was Roy Dexheimer, and his son was about six or seven years old. That little kid used to crack up over that routine.

"I also had a radio show there in Springfield in 1935, on WTAX. There was a white drummer named Barry Dean who used to come into the studio sometimes and drum on the chairs and the walls while I'd be playing.

"I left Springfield after a few months and went to Decatur, Illinois. Then I went to Peoria, where I stayed at this ofay hotel, the Jefferson. I was the first black ever to stay there, and I stayed there because I was working at the hotel. Now, a lot of black entertainers wouldn't have dared try to stay in a white hotel, even if they were appearing there. But my attitude was, 'Look, I'm working here, and I'm going to stay here.'

"Peoria was a wide-open town in those days, and the Jefferson was downtown, right in the middle of the action. I didn't go in for all that notorious stuff, though. I went about my business.

"Then, still in 1935, I joined a group called Jerry Lynch and His Band, out of Champaign, Illinois. I was with them for quite a while, too. We mostly played dancing rooms."

When the music business "got bad," and he couldn't get

work either as a single or with a group, Scatman worked as a bellhop and porter—"anything to make an honest living."

While he was working quite steadily and making good money, his penchant for gambling caused him to be short of cash from time to time. On one occasion, he was forced to hock his guitar, which meant he couldn't do his regular routine. According to Les Wolf, whose father owned a clothing store at 631 Wabash Avenue, Scatman went to the store to ask for a loan so he could get his guitar out of hock. They gave him the money, on the condition that he entertain at a party at one Pete Van Horn's cabin. At the party, Scatman got into a crap game and won big, breaking just about everyone else.

Soon Scatman was back on the road in the role of itinerant entertainer. In the South, they would have said he had "travel dust" in his shoes. He worked with a variety of groups, but never stayed with any of them for long. Whenever possible, he worked as a single, for he liked being his own boss and the freedom that gave him to move around as he wanted. He was never in one place for long.

By 1936, Scatman had traveled and worked with a variety of bands, and it occurred to him that he could manage a band as well as anyone else: "I decided I'm going to get me a band. I organized this five-piece band—bass drum, piano, trumpet, sax, drums. On piano I had Duke Crowder, who is a principal of a high school in Cincinnati now. Jimmy Harris was on sax. My drummer, Charles Cardwell, died a long time ago. And then I got Sam the Man Taylor, out of Alabama State College. He was big in Japan years ago. When I was back in New York in '81 doing this movie, we had just gotten back from Europe and I went to the hospital to see him. He was seventeen when I sent for him, just a kid. He and Jimmy Harris were blowing then what they're playing now. That's how advanced my band was. And I was no bad drummer myself.

"I called the band Scat Man and His Band. I didn't have any bookings lined up, but I figured I could get some jobs. So, we went to Paris, Illinois, about twenty miles from Terre Haute, and

I asked where was the nearest nightclub and was directed to this Caucasian club called the Trees.

"I walked in and said, 'I want you to hear my band.' They said okay, we played, and we got the job. The first week or two I didn't see how the man was going to pay us, but he did pay us. But word got around. I didn't know nothing about PR men in those days. All my advertising was mouth to mouth. We worked at this club for nearly a year, and we packed them in there, we really packed them in there. By the time we left, every night was like New Year's Eve. I think I was paying the cats fourteen dollars a week, and I think I was making twenty-five. That was good money in those days, when room and board wasn't but two dollars a week. When we left that club, the musicians had rolls of money."

Harry Frye, who later became administrative assistant to Mayor Pete Chalos, was performing in bands at that time. "Scatman was very popular. He was quite a showman, and he was just very well liked. He drew a crowd every place he played. He was a singer, and he did a little dancing, a little comic stuff—a general entertainer more than a straight musician.

"Of the black bands, his was the most popular. We were not into mixed bands in those days. You had two or three black bands, and the rest were white."

Most black performers in the 1930s had to work for black clubs—small honky-tonks or juke joints—and the occasional big-city black theater. In the theaters, the preferred fare was vaudeville, and in order to get bookings you had to go through the Theatre Owners Booking Agency (TOBA). Scatman never went that route.

"I worked very few black places; I can count them on one hand. No vaudeville. None of that. Just working in exclusive nightclubs, ofay hotels. One time I disorganized my band, and I started just strolling with my guitar in different first-rate hotels. I was the first black cat to ever do that. From table to table with my guitar. That's called 'strollin'. I worked there in Dayton, Ohio, at the Wagon Wheel, just strolling with my guitar. I also worked the Biltmore."

The only places where he performed for blacks were the "black and tans," interracial clubs, always owned by whites, that featured jazz entertainment and catered to the more adventurous sorts in both races who had to look harder for their adventure now that Prohibition had been repealed and the speakeasies no longer had their reason to exist. At the black and tans, the races could come together, and sometimes even mingled, a social experience they could not get otherwise—and that was made possible in part by jazz.

"It must have been after we left Paris that we did a gig in Canton, Ohio," Scatman continued. "We were at a club called the Commodore, a black and tan, and we were there for several months. The first time I met my wife, Helen, was in Canton in 1936. I'll never forget that. She was the prettiest little girl I'd ever laid eyes on. I couldn't wait to get back to Canton on the chance that I'd see her again.

"Then we went to Dayton. At that time, I had two of those big old beautiful 1931 Cadillacs—one to carry the band and one for the instruments and luggage. If I knew then what I know now, I'd have kept those Cadillacs. They're worth a fortune now.

"In Dayton I had Jimmy Harris on alto, Johnny Letman from Chicago on trumpet, Charles Cardwell on drums, and Duke Crowder on the piano. Later on, Snooky Young joined us because Johnny had to go somewhere. Snooky was about seventeen years old, and he was blowing then. We used to call him Mouse. Now, he works with Doc Severinsen. A few years back, I recorded my 'Mean Dog Blues' for a jazz album he was putting out. When Snooky came into the band, we were working at a white club called the Chesame. It was a beautiful club, but they didn't do that much business. I told the guy, 'You want to make some money? Change this into a black and tan. Call it the Swing Club.' He did, and he started packing them in, black and white. I'd get on that floor and do a forty-five, fifty-minute show just with me and the band."

Among their routines was one about the Numbers, one of the most popular of the many Scatman created in the 1930s. Scatman was a confirmed player of the Numbers. "I had my dream book and everything, played the Numbers every day for most of my life. I was so into playing the Numbers that I even made a routine out of it for my band. We did it nearly every night. This is how it went:

"Hey, nanny, nanny, what you say?
I've got a number for today
Where did you get it at, where did you get it at?
Over the telephone, like Big Ben told all of his men
Don't you take no Numbers after half past ten
Half past ten, I can't win
I got a way you can slip it in
Well, you take them down to the spot and they don't
    turn them in until twelve o'clock
Here's everybody's numbers for your inspection
I'll damn sho take in your collection
What's that? That's three
What's that? That's six
What's this? That's nine
What's the matter, man, you blowing your mind
You know what three, six, nine is?
That road is a shady road
What's the matter, man, you're losing your life?
Ain't going to play it, here's a light
Play it for a dollar
Oh, the boss might holler
Play it for a half
Aw, don't make me laugh
Take a drink of water and play it for a quarter
Are you going to be a hog before you commence?
Well, put me down for fifteen cents
Now you're stepping the righteous path,
You play it for a quarter, and I'll play it for a half
Because we're going to hit the number."

Playing the Numbers, playing his guitar, entertaining folks, being able to buy a new suit when he wanted to—that was happiness for Scatman. That his life did not have much focus did not bother him at all. He had no big dreams. He just wanted to make a living doing what he enjoyed, which was bringing enjoyment to other people. He was a hard worker and a hustler for jobs, but he liked his relaxation, too. He played the Numbers religiously, read his Bible, and took up weed thanks to some of his musician friends. He was hardly alone in that habit. Many other musicians, among them Louis Armstrong, smoked reefer to relax. "It's good for everything," Scatman liked to say. "It makes you think beautifully. It's just good for you. There's a saying in the Bible that I always relate to, 'In all of your getting, get good understanding.' "

The one thing he wanted but did not have was a steady woman. He had travel dust in his heart as well as in his shoes, and Scatman had his lady friends in the various cities and towns where he performed. But by 1936, he had been on the road for seven years, and he was looking for a steadier life. He still enjoyed traveling, but he wanted a wife to share his life with him. The woman he married would share his life for almost fifty years.

CHAPTER 3

YOU AND ME AGAINST THE WORLD

HELEN SULLIVAN WAS BORN AND RAISED IN STEUBENVILLE, Ohio. "We're Hungarian, so Sullivan is kind of a stupid name," she says. "Our name was Sullivardi, or something like that, and everybody had a hard time pronouncing it, so my oldest brother went and had it changed. It was stupid to change it to an Irish name, but that's what we've been going by all these years."

Helen was one of thirteen children. A grandmother also lived with them, so there were sixteen people in the household. Her father worked in the steel mills, shoveling coal into the furnace. Her mother spent most of her time seeing to the meals for the large family and doing a superb job of it. Helen recalls, "My father used to say, 'We may not be wealthy, but we're healthy.'

"My brother and father used to carry hundred-pound sacks of flour and sugar on their backs up the hill, because when my mother made bread, she'd make it in one of those old-fashioned tubs you washed clothes in. She'd put a clean tablecloth in it, and she'd fill up two or three of those with bread dough, and make biscuits and all, and in two days everything would be gone because we were such a big family.

"We had a big garden. We didn't have a horse to plow, but they used to take a pitchfork and till the soil, and as far as you could see, the rows would be perfectly straight. We had huge tomatoes, corn, cabbage. My father had a long shredder, and he used to shred cabbage and make barrels of sauerkraut. We picked blueberries and blackberries, and my father would make huckleberry wine. We had apple trees, and my mother used to make apple butter. She made ketchup from the tomatoes, pickle relish from the cucumbers.

"The only things we had to buy were flour and sugar, and coffee and tea. My mother and father would go around and sell tomatoes for fifty cents a basket, and there would be about thirty tomatoes in the basket."

There were fields to roam, trees to climb. "I remember my father fixed up a swing for us in an apple tree." Always, there were plenty of people around for company, and Helen does not recall ever feeling overwhelmed by so much family. She loved helping her mother bake bread and pick berries. Helen was a doer, and there was always plenty to do. "Looking back, I had a great childhood . . . until I had to go to school.

"I did not like school. The first time my mother took me to school, I was scared, and when they had recess, I went back home. My brother took me back because I was so scared."

School was full of strangers, and rules. Helen couldn't run through the fields or swing under the apple tree or talk and laugh when she felt like it. At school, stern teachers made her sit still and punished her when she talked and scolded her when they caught her looking out the window, longing for freedom.

"I used to play hookey all the time. One time my girlfriend and I decided we didn't want to go to school, so we dug a hole by the road and buried our books in it. Then we went to the movie show downtown. We were sitting in the show when it started to rain, and by the time we got back and dug up the books, they were all muddy. You talk about catching hell!"

Eventually, the local priest suggested that Helen go into a convent school, where she would get an education and learn skills she would need later to get a job. Her parents thought it would be a good idea, and so did Helen, who by this time had argued with her parents about school so often that she had also decided she wanted to get away from home. So, at age nine, Helen enrolled at the Home of the Good Shepherd convent school in Columbus.

"Boy, they were sure religious," she says. "I had to go the church every morning—*every* morning. I didn't like that, but I did like the practical training they gave me at the school.

"I learned to sew there. They had a shirt factory. I learned to run all the machines. I used to do the button strips, make the collar points. The only thing I didn't do was sew up the sides of the shirts and put on the collars. A couple of years later, they made me inspector. I used to go around inspecting all the materials because some of the girls wanted to make the stitches bigger so they'd get more work done. Everybody had a quota to do, and you had to keep those stitches real small on those shirts because otherwise they'd just burst open.

"After I married Scat, my sewing skills came in handy; I was always mending uniforms, sewing on buttons. And after my daughter, Donna, was born, I was always sewing for her."

Helen completed high school at the convent, but once she was graduated, she didn't stay around. She had no intention of following a religious vocation. What she wanted was to get a job, but not in Steubenville. She had no desire to stay in her hometown like most of her siblings. One of her sisters worked as a waitress at the Three Step Inn, which was owned by Dean Martin's father. "You had to walk up three steps to get to it, so that's how it got its name. It was just a little joint that sold beer and wine, and guys from the mill used to go there. Dean used to sing in the club for nothing."

Helen, who before entering the convent school had often gone to the movies instead of to class, had the idea of going into show business. She could sing and dance a little, and had a winning personality. She was also seventeen years old, blond, and possessed of a healthy, corn-fed beauty. One of her girl-friends had also decided on a show-business career.

"There was a carnival in town, and she went up there," says Helen, "and she came back and said they were looking for girls. All we had to do was wear a little bra and G-string. She said, 'Listen, I want to get away from here,' and I did, too. I didn't want to end up a poor farmer.

"So we went over there and talked to a guy, and he said he needed someone that night. I was kind of afraid that someone who knew me would see me, but I went ahead. They taught us a little dance with a chair: 'Howdy-do, everybody, howdy-do. We're here to sing and do a dance for you. We hope you like our style. We hope you like our smile. Howdy-do, everybody, howdy-do.' Then we were supposed to sit down and cross our legs.

"So, we did the first show, and who comes by but my uncle, who was Hungarian and could hardly speak a word of English. He went home and told my father, and my father came down there. He shook his fist at me and was yelling at me in Hungarian—I'd been away so long, I'd forgotten how to speak it, but I understood exactly what he was saying. He was telling me wait until I got home. Well, I never did go home. The carnival was leaving town that night, and my girlfriend and I got on the train and left with it.

"We went to Indiana next. One night I was having trouble getting the bra on, and the guy who ran the show came by and said, 'Why don't you just go on without it. You can see through it anyway.' I told him I wasn't going out on that stage with nothing on top, and he said I'd go out there or else. So I quit. I quit, and I didn't have any place to go.

"The guy gave me the few bucks that he owed me, and so I went back to the convent. I only stayed there two nights. I told the head nun that I wasn't going to stay. I met a girl there who was getting ready to leave. She gave me her address, and I went and stayed at her house for a while. I even got a job as a waitress. But then I met this other girl named Jean, whom I knew from before, and we went to Canton, Ohio, where she had relatives and where we could stay while we looked for jobs.

"I got a little job as a waitress, but I was still staying with Jean. She kept asking me to go with her to this club called the Commodore, which was a black-and-tan club. I had never been to a black-and-tan club, and the strongest thing I was drinking was Coke, but one night I said, 'Okay.' Jean was going with the saxophone player in Scat's band, but I didn't know it at the time. When we got there, she introduced me to him—his name was Jimmy—and then Jimmy called Scat over and introduced us, and I don't know, it must have been love at first sight. It was April 1936.

"He was wearing long white tails, and a bow tie, and he was sharp. He emceed the show, and played his drums and guitar, and sang, and then his band would play. It was a real big show. He asked me to dance, and we were dancing, and I was standing way far away from him. He said, 'I'm not gonna bite you. You can get a little closer.' We danced and danced and danced.

"No one said anything about it, really. They were used to going to those kinds of clubs—black and tans—and seeing people of different races dance together. Even if anyone had objected, it wouldn't have mattered to me. I was only seventeen years old, but I made up my mind. I said to myself, 'This is the man I want, this is the man I'm gonna have.'

"So then, after that, every night I'd try to go down there to the club. And that went on for about three weeks, until he had to leave. I said, 'Oh, God, I hope he comes back. If he doesn't, I'm gonna hire a private detective.' I kept thinking about him and thinking about him.

"A few months later, he came back. He called me and asked if he could see me before he went to work that night, and I went down there and we hugged and kissed. This was around seven o'clock. Then, later, I went to the club for the ten o'clock show. This went on for a while, me going to the club every night. I made all kinds of excuses to the people I was staying with. They were white, and I didn't know how they would feel about me going to see him.

"The place had three floors. There was a big Greek restaurant downstairs, rooms on the second floor, and then on the third floor was the club. Scat had a room there, and of all places it was right next to the ladies' room. So during intermission, I would go to the ladies' room, and he would be in his room. He'd say, 'Come in, I'm not going to hurt you.' I'd go in and sit on the bed and we'd talk. He didn't put his arm around me or anything, he was such a gentleman. I think that's really what drew me to him. It made me care for him more and more.

"When he went away again, I missed him so much. He missed me, too, so we decided to get married. He was playing in Akron, and I was still in Canton, staying with the same people. He got his blood test in Akron, and I got mine in Canton. Then he came back to Canton, and we went to the courthouse to get married. The date was July 15, 1937.

"When we went to the courthouse, you'd have thought a three-ring circus had come to town. Everybody had their heads out windows looking at us. I was young and looked pretty good in those days, and he was handsome and well dressed, but they weren't looking at us because we were good-looking.

"I was wearing dark glasses. They told me to take them off. They saw that I had bluish-green eyes. Then, the judge said he couldn't marry us. He said it was because we had got our blood tests in two different places. Well, you know that was just an excuse—we both got our blood tests in Ohio. So we walked out. Everybody was looking at us, but we just ignored them. If that had happened today, we could have sued them. But then, we didn't want any arguments. Or at least Scat didn't. I'm the one who was standing there saying 'What difference does it make, it's in Ohio?' But Scat just said, 'All right,' and escorted me out.

"Later, some friends of ours took us to Cleveland, and we got married there."

Scatman loved to say of his interracial marriage, "I did it before it was fashionable." Helen agrees that they were pioneers of a sort. "Later on in years, after he became famous, people started admiring us. Even in the early years, there were some people who treated us well—really well. But the majority of whites didn't think much of interracial marriages. We tried to just ignore anyone who said anything."

Scatman recalled that occasionally someone wanted to know how he had the courage to marry Helen: "Some black cat says, 'Hey, man, you married to a white woman?' I says, 'Yeah, why?' And he says, 'What's them cats gonna do to you for that?' And I says, 'They ain't gonna bother us 'cause we don't make no big, flauntin' issue of it.' I was never the type to show her off, that was my private life. When my wife came to see the show, she'd be just another customer, and when I got off from work, we'd go home together. See, we weren't trying to show off. We were never on an ego trip."

Helen remembers, "My family was a little bit shocked at first, but they accepted Scat, and they came to love him. My parents were really good people, who were not prejudiced. I grew up in a mixed neighborhood. The first bath I ever took in a bathtub was at these black people's house. We had those old-fashioned tubs that you washed clothes in, and that's what we used to bathe in, because we were poor. And I still remember that first bath in a bathtub. There was myself and this little black girl and this little Mexican girl, and another white girl. We thought we were in heaven, sitting in a bathtub.

"My father worked with black men at the mill, shoveling coal into the furnaces. I remember him telling me how the handle of the shovel would get hot, and there was this black fellow there who couldn't even afford to buy a fifteen-cent pair of gloves. My father took and bought some gloves for him.

"My mother was so good-hearted. These hoboes used to come to our house and ask for food. She used to tell them to sit on the steps, and although we were poor ourselves, she'd go in and make butter and jelly sandwiches and take them out to them, and give them coffee.

"So that's how I was raised up—to love everybody and treat everybody right."

"My parents never met Scat, although he talked to my mother on the phone a lot. My sisters and brothers have."

*   *   *

Scatman's parents never got to meet Helen. His mother died in 1937, and his father died the following year. "They tell me," said Scatman in 1986, "that one night he went to bed and never woke up."

Helen recalls, "It was a shock to him. He was real sad. But he had the kind of mind that didn't let sadness linger. He thought about how happy he was with me, or what a good life he had, and got over it. So the sadness didn't stay with him a long time. A few years later—it was about four years after I met him—we had to go through his hometown of Terre Haute, Indiana, on the way somewhere. We stopped and stayed with his sister, Frances, just for the night. The other sisters and the brother came over, and I met them."

Helen says that Scatman's siblings never really accepted her. "In later years, he'd tell them to call him and reverse the charges," she says, "but they complained that I always answered the phone. We didn't have too much to do with them. They only came around when they wanted something from him."

Ironically, Scatman's relatives were among the few blacks who did not accept their interracial union. Most other blacks adopted a live-and-let-live attitude. Some thought Scatman crazy to take his life into his hands that way. Some wondered why Helen would choose the hard road of life with a black man when she clearly could have married any number of white men.

But the general attitude among blacks was that what they did was their own business, and Helen can recall little black hostility in those early years. Her recollections are filled with instances of kindness from black people, in whose neighborhoods and hotels and homes she would, as Scatman's wife, live for the next thirty years or more.

"Looking back, we really didn't have many problems," Helen says. "Anyway, we were so happy that we didn't let other people bother us. Forty-nine years and we never had a fight. We would disagree about things, but later I'd go up to him and put my arms around him and say, 'Honey, I was wrong.' Or he'd

come up to me and say, 'Honey, you were right again!' No dragging each other down or anything like that."

But Helen admits to being jealous of the women who hung
around her Scat. "He had a lot of girlfriends before me," she
says. "I knew that, and it didn't bother me. But all those girls
who used to come around, those hangers-on—they call them
groupies now—that did bother me.The guys in the band were
very attractive fellows, and there were always girls. I remember
in Akron, Scat's car broke down, and this girl used to come and
pick him up every night and take him to the theater or wherever
he was playing, and then bring him home. I told him I didn't like
that, but he'd just say, 'Aw, honey, she's just being nice.'

"They'd send him things—robes and things like that. I remember once, in Pittsburgh, this girl sent him pajamas and a
robe. I said, 'How come this girl is sending you a present like
that?' He said she was just being nice. I told him, 'I don't know
what you're doing, and I don't want to know. But I do know I
don't want this robe and pajamas in my house.' I threw them in
the garbage. I was so jealous of Scat. I didn't want another
woman to even come near him."

Over the years, Helen learned to view the hangers-on as a
necessary evil. She had an attractive, talented, nice man, and she
couldn't blame the other girls for wanting him. But she was
secure enough in his love for her that she was no longer afraid
of losing him.

A radio interviewer once asked Scatman if he'd ever been
tempted to stray. "Oh, I've been tempted, just like Jesus Christ
was tempted," Scatman answered. "But my baby's home. I look
at the garden, she knows that. But I always go home and take
care of the business."

By the time Helen and Scatman were married, he had established his headquarters in Akron, Ohio, and had a steady gig.
He recalled, "I had nine pieces in my band then, and we were
working this club called Harry's Black and Tan. Leonard Firestone used to come out there once or twice a week with a nice
party. He'd say, 'Why don't you come out to the club and I'll

teach you how to play golf.' I said, 'Thank you, Leonard, but I don't play that silly game.' "

Years later, Scatman became a veritable golf addict.

According to Helen, after they were married, Scatman went into the Kit Kat Club. He was staying at the Green Turtle Hotel, a black hotel in Akron, and Helen moved in. "They were really nice people there," Helen recalls. "I spoke to everybody." She remembers, "He was making around a hundred-fifty dollars a week, and the guys were making about seventy-five a week. Every Sunday night he'd go to Cleveland to play at Oster's ballroom. It was packed every Sunday night, they just waited for him to come."

At Oster's ballroom, Scatman met up with his old friend Sulky Davis, with whom he had played at the Luscious Place speakeasy back in Terre Haute. Davis proceeded to write a theme song for Scatman, which he used for the rest of his life: "I am the Scat Man/if you don't know who I am/I'll tell you a story that you'll understand. . . ."

"After that," says Helen, "we traveled all over Ohio, playing wherever Scat could get jobs. I didn't travel with him—not for the first couple of years, anyway. It wouldn't have been very smart, with the racial climate the way it was. He and the fellows would go ahead in the two cars. I'd take the bus or a train and join them wherever they were playing. He didn't have an agent. He would just go to a club or hotel, ask to see the manager, and ask for an audition. A lot of times, they got the job."

Said Scatman years later, "I wish I'd known then what I know now. I would have gotten me an agent, but I wasn't too hip in those days. I booked myself."

Scatman had a five-piece band then. They covered the state of Ohio—Cincinnati, Cleveland, Canton, Akron, Dayton— taking whatever engagements they could get.

"Sometimes," says Helen, "the band got a chance to play down South, but I wouldn't go with Scat. Not with all the prejudice down there. In some of those places down South, black people had to be off the streets by eight or nine o'clock. I said, 'No way am I going down there with you,' and I wouldn't go to those places. I never did go down South with Scat, not even in the 1970s and eighties. Sometime in the 1980s he went down South for a golf tournament. The governor had invited Scat and all the other celebrities to his mansion for dinner. Scat tried to get me to go, but I said, 'No way. I am not going down South with you.'

"The furthest South I ever went with him was Arkansas, and I can remember we had a few unpleasant incidents there.

"Can you imagine what would have happened if Scat had brought a white wife down South in those days? Whites down there wouldn't even let black people say 'white beans.' You had to say 'navy beans.' "

Traveling in the South had not got any easier for blacks since Scatman had last been there on tour with Montague's Serenaders. Once again, places where they could eat a solid meal were few and far between, hotel accommodations were lacking, and they had bus troubles. Scatman remembered traveling in Texas most vividly.

"One time we were in Dallas. I was walking down the street, and it was nine-thirty or ten o'clock. I'd just had a meal, and I mean a real meal. I even remember the name of the restaurant, Cushenberry's. I was feeling good, and here comes this motorcycle cop. He says, 'Hey, where you going, nigger?' I said, 'Power Hotel.' He said, 'Well, okay, get on off the street.' I said, 'Yes sir.' I didn't let that kind of thing bother me, because I knew things were going to get better. But you had to keep alert when you drove into a town like Denison, Texas, where the sign read it was the home of 'the blackest earth and the whitest people' in all Texas.

"Another time, in Tyler, Texas, the bus broke down, and these white guys came on. They started asking all sorts of questions—'Where you from, *boy?*' 'Where you going, *boy?*' And some of our cats, they started getting chesty, sassing back. Well, those white folks were just about to *burn* that bus.

"But I got up and said, 'Look, my friends here are from the North. They don't understand how to act. Please forgive them. See, I was born and raised here ('course I lied). Sure would appreciate it if you didn't harm that bus.' I just humbled myself, and they let us go. Today, they'd call that Uncle Tomming, but that wasn't any Uncle Tomming. That was just knowing what to do at the right time. Like the Bible says, 'He that shall humble himself shall be exalted.'

"I never really had a bad time in those days, 'cause I knew, 'When in Rome, do as the Romans do.' So, I knew what to do and when to do it. My gift of gab kept me out of trouble a lot. and I never let things like that dwell in my heart. I'd just forget it, 'cause I knew they didn't know . . . I never let anger rest in my bosom.

"What I liked about those people was that you didn't find no phonies down there. If they liked you, they really liked you. If they didn't like you, they did not mess with you. The only ones that hated black people was the ones that were threatened, and the only ones that was threatened was the ones that had less. So you had to be careful. But you couldn't stay closed.

"One time, a white guy came up to me and said, 'You're a good nigger. Now, when you have intermission, why don't you come and have a drink with me.' I said, 'Okay.' When intermission came, I went over, and he took out his flask and gave it to me. I took a drink. He said, 'I'm not even going to wipe it off.' I said, 'Thank you.' He really liked me. He called me 'nigger,' but didn't mean it in a derogatory way, that's all he knew."

The band was glad to get back to the Midwest, however. Audiences were equally appreciative, and you didn't have to watch your back so much. Scatman was delighted to get back to Helen, for whom he literally ached when they had to be apart. The aching parts of his body did not include his stomach, however, for Helen couldn't cook—at least not at first. Scatman, on the other hand, loved to eat:

> I must have been behind the door
> the day they passed out brains
> I don't even know enough to
> come in when it rains
> In school I'm a fool

At work I'm a jerk
And at play I'm all hands and feet
But—when I sit down to eat
I don't take no backseat
cause . . . I'm . . . the . . .
only-man-in-the-world-who-can-take-a-biscuit-apart
and put it back together like it was
And if you doubt what I'm saying
Ask the lady where I'm staying
If I don't or if I does
Now Rudolph Valentino had a lot of fun
But what he did to women, I can do to a bun
Cause I'm the
Only-man-in-the-world-who-can-take-a-biscuit-apart
And put it back together like it was
Yes I'm the only gentleman on this planet
Who can take a muffin
And restore it to its original state
And you even have my permission
To ask my physician if I prevaricate
Now I visited the Mayo Clinic
And they gave me a piece of bread
They turned the X-ray on me
And then the Mayo brothers said
Yes, you're the
Only man in the world who can take a biscuit apart
And put it back together like it was.

Helen says, "Now, before I met Scat, I couldn't boil water. I didn't know what black-eye peas and neckbones were. I looked at him like he was crazy when he said, 'I'd like some black-eye peas and neckbones.' But I got a cookbook, and my mother sent me another cookbook, and I started learning how to cook. I got to be a very good cook."

Her skill at cooking came in very handy in the lean times, of which there were many in the early years. The engagements that paid Scatman $150 a week and his sidemen $75 were comparatively few. Helen recalls a stint in Akron, Ohio, around 1939–40: "They'd be out of work two or three weeks at a time. Scat would be worried about the boys working. The fellows would be wondering where their rent was coming from. I figured I could at least feed them."

"We were living in a hotel, and I had this little burner, and I bought one plate, one cup, one saucer, one knife, one fork, one spoon. I had one little coffeepot. I would go to the store, and I'd come back with beans and greens and a loaf of bread, some butter and some coffee. And I'd cook. Thank God our room looked out onto an alley so the manager couldn't smell my cooking those beans and greens and stuff. I'd try to situate the burner so the smoke and steam would blow out the window.

"Then I'd send for each of the guys in the band, one by one. One would eat, and then I'd wash out that cup and saucer and that plate and I'd say, 'So-and-so, when you go out, you send so-and-so in. I'd do that until all of them were fed, and then Scat would sit down and eat, and then finally I would. We had some tough days.

"Then finally he would find a weekend job, maybe paying ten dollars a night for three nights. So we'd pay a week's rent, which was four dollars, and then we'd feed eight in a restaurant and buy gas for the cars, and then we'd be broke again. We couldn't save anything.

"It was a struggle. Sometimes, the money we'd get wouldn't even pay the bills. But I'd pay a little bit here and a little bit there. I was very good at budgeting. I used to go and buy a whole outfit for ten dollars—a dress for three-ninety-eight, a hat for seventy-nine cents, a pair of shoes for a dollar, stockings for twenty-nine cents, purse for thirty-nine cents, pair of gloves for twenty-nine cents. I'd have a complete outfit for ten dollars, and I'd look good. Today, that outfit would cost you a hundred and fifty dollars.

"Scat and I always liked to look good. Even if I was just going to the grocery store, I had on my hat and gloves. I was always dressed up. I had three suits, and a lot of accessories to change the outfit."

Even when times were lean, Scatman would not hear of Helen's getting a job to help out: "He said, 'I don't want you working. You're not supposed to work. I'm the man, and I'll take care of you. And that's the way it always was. He never got depressed. He never felt like giving up. He'd say, 'Don't worry, honey, everything's gonna be all right.' And it would be, you know? But I do feel he was a workaholic. When he could get work, he worked three jobs at a time. Because he never knew when he would be out of work."

At one point, while they were in Dayton, Scatman could not take the responsibility of finding work for a five-piece band any longer. He disbanded the group and went solo for a time. "One of the fellows got a job offer with another band," says Helen, "and Scat said, 'Go on and take it.' He was very good about that. He always had the musicians' best interests in mind. He paid them above scale, which is why so many of them stayed with him so long.

"A lot of orchestra leaders don't want to show the talents of the musicians. Scat wasn't like that. He had a piano player who could really sing, and he would let him sing a lot of songs. And then he taught them all how to sing together."

But for Scatman, the musician's leaving seemed to signal the time to break up the band and go solo for a while. "He had a job at a very exclusive dinner place," says Helen, "and he would just stroll around the tables with his guitar, singing songs to people. They really loved it. He did that for quite a while."

Scatman was successful enough to hire an agent in Akron. Earl Mills would later represent Dorothy Dandridge.

But Scatman really wanted to be a bandleader, and as soon as he could, he formed a bigger band, this time with seven pieces, plus a girl singer, since "girl singers" were *de rigueur* for big bands in those wartime years when ballads were so popular.

"He was a good bandleader," says Helen. "He had them practice all the time. He would fine them for being late. He would give them first time late, and then the second time he would fine them five dollars, third time more—because you have a room full of people waiting for the music, and if somebody's not there, that's pretty bad.

"He paid them a fair wage—more than a fair wage. He showcased them. Some of the musicians stayed with him fifteen or twenty years.

"A lot of times they worked places where there were gamblers, and they got good tips. Scat had this kitty, and gangsters used to come in and put hundred-dollar bills in there. At the end of the night, instead of splitting the tips, Scat would let the boys know how much it was and how much each of them were entitled to. And then he would bring it home, and I would keep it. I'd put it in the bank. Then, if anything came up—like one of the boy's cars broke down or they needed new uniforms—we would use the tips. A lot of them would come to me when they needed room rent, or for whatever they needed, and I'd give them the money. The bank account was in my name and Scat's, but I kept track of how much each fellow had. Later on, after Scat broke up the band and started getting into pictures, they all had a nice sum of money coming.

"Juanita Brown was the girl singer in those days. She was the only one who kept her tips. She had to buy her gowns. She used to go to the secondhand stores and get the most beautiful gowns, five-hundred-dollar gowns for fifty dollars. She always looked nice."

Scat Man and his Band tried the East Coast for a time, playing successfully at the Sportsmans' Inn owned by Ray Fine in Cohoes, near Albany, New York. Scatman loved to tell the story of his first meeting with Fine.

"We drove up to this club, and I asked to see the manager, and old Ray Fine said, 'I'm the manager.' I said, 'Look, I've got a band, and I'd like you to hear it.' He said, 'I've already got a band.' I said, 'That's all right, I want you to hear my band.' Helen was sitting in the car, and he said, 'Who's that girl?' I said, 'That's my wife. Contrast.' He got a big kick out of that. Not only did he give me the job, but every year from then on he sent birthday cards and Christmas cards that just said, 'Dear Scatman, or Dear Scatman and Helen, Contrast.'

"It was a beautiful club, and there was a revolving band-stand in the middle of the bar, and they just loved us there. We must have played there two or three years."

After the engagement at the Sportsman's Inn, Scat Man and His Band got their first booking through an agent, in Albany proper. "By that time," according to Scatman, "I had nine pieces, ten with the girl vocalist. We were doing then what cats are doing now. Honest. I always told the cats, 'We got to do more than play, we gotta entertain, sing, make people happy.'"

While they were in the Albany area, Scatman suggested to his musicians that they try to get a gig at the Savoy Ballroom in Harlem, which at the time was famous for its battles of the bands. The Savoy Sultans were the resident band at the time, soon to be replaced by Chick Webb and His Orchestra, featuring the teenage singer Ella Fitzgerald. Scatman was convinced that his group could match the best the Savoy had to offer, "But the boys in the band were a little shy. I know good and well we could have blown those Savoy Sultans out of the bandstand. I had a band that was chicken. In later years, they came back to me and told me, 'Yeah, man, you were right.' Even Sam the Man Taylor, who later made his home base in New York, said that. I said, 'I know I was right, but everything happens for the best.'"

Helen recalls, "We stayed in Albany at the time—in this black lady's rooming house. We checked in at night, and she called Scat up and said, 'Now, before your wife goes out tomorrow, have her put some dark brown powder on her face so they'll think she's black.' Scat told her, 'This is my wife. She's white. She can't help it, just like I can't help being black. She's not gonna put nothin' on her face, she's gonna go as she is.'

"Most of the time, black people treated us very well. They treated me like a queen. There wasn't the resentment against mixed couples in the black community that there is now. That is the only time in the early days that I can remember any black person making us feel uncomfortable.

"I remember when we stayed in Cincinnati, we rented a room from this lady who used to rent rooms to all the black entertainers. One time when we were there, she had twelve female impersonators staying in her rooms. They used to dress up in their little dresses and high heels and strut around the house. They were real nice. And the lady who owned the house treated me nicely. She used to bring coffee up to the room and invite me down to have meals, and she just liked to talk to me.

"Of course, it was also in Cincinnati that I got stopped by the police one time. Scat had let me off in a white neighborhood to go shopping or something. This police car drove up, and the cops asked me what was I doing with a nigger. I said, 'He's my husband.' They said, 'You're white, and he's a nigger.' I said, 'No, I'm not white. I'm colored.' One of them said, 'You look white to me.' I said, 'I'm just light, but I'm colored.' He said, 'Well, go on back down there with your people where you belong.' I went. I got a cab and came on back home, because I didn't want to go to jail. Scat laughed his behind off when I told him that. He said, 'Go on back up there with your people. Don't be coming down here.' "

In 1943, Scatman, accompanied by a four-piece band consisting of Jimmy Harris on alto sax, Milton Thomas on trumpet, Lee Barnes on piano, and Sylvester Turpin on bass, played an engagement at the Beachcomber in Omaha, Nebraska, that was so successful that some PR man called it a "gross buster." The band was subsequently offered a holdover engagement.

While in Omaha, they also met up with Louis Armstrong. "We stayed in the same room-and-board house together," Helen recalls. "He was there with his wife at the time, and he and Scat were good friends. They were always laughing and joking and clowning. They had a ball all the time. Every time we went down to eat, they had that poor old lady who ran the boardinghouse in tears, laughing at the things they said.

"Louis was just coming up then. People knew who he was, but he wasn't as famous as in years to come. Scat thought he was the greatest person. In fact, he used to do a song where he imitated Louis."

Armstrong, ten years Scatman's senior, was already well known in international music circles and had toured extensively in Europe. At the time, his career was at a comparative standstill, due in part to his arrest in 1939 on a marijuana charge. It was no secret that many jazzmen smoked reefer. Scatman had smoked marijuana since the late 1920s and was in the habit of carrying a couple of reefers in his socks. He just hadn't been caught. Helen remembers a time years later when they drove down to Mexico from Los Angeles and he gave her a couple of reefers just before they crossed the border. After that, she refused to go to Mexico with him. Scatman said he smoked marijuana because it made him think beautiful thoughts. Armstrong said he smoked marijuana as an insulator against the pain of racism. Armstrong had also got in the middle of a fight between mobs for control of his Chicago venues, and he was at that time staying away from both Chicago and New York. Within a few years, however, he would be an international superstar. Scatman had years more dues to pay before his name became a household word. But at least his career was about to take a successful turn.

CHAPTER 4

FROM CHICAGO TO HOLLYWOOD

BY THE TIME THEY WENT TO OMAHA, Scatman had an agent in Chicago named Bert Gervis, whose offices were at 203 N. Wabash. Gervis had approached Scatman about representing the band, and Scatman was doing quite well financially and felt he could afford to pay for some publicity.

Gervis used the success of Scat Man and His Band in Omaha to get the group booked into the Capitol Lounge in the Windy City in September 1943. There, they were so successful that they made the rounds of the Loop, returning more than once to the Capitol Lounge. "They had five ofay clubs right in the Loop," according to Scatman. "They had the Capitol Lounge, the Brass Rail, the Band Box, the Hollywood Showboat, and the Rumba Casino, all in the Loop. I worked all those clubs. Then I worked a club on the South Side for Ed White called Café de Society, 309 East Garfield Boulevard. We used to broadcast over WIND five nights a week, Monday and Wednesday through Saturday, at eleven forty five P.M. I had Oliver Michaux on piano, Jimmy Harris on alto, Turk on bass, and I was on drums. Milton Thomas left the band around that time, and I hired Leroy Nabors to play trumpet."

By this time, Scat Man and His Band were playing bop, a new musical form popularized by alto saxophonist Charlie Parker, trumpeter Dizzy Gillespie, pianist Thelonious Monk, and others. Considered the first modern jazz style, it was a development from swing, but unlike swing was primarily a combo style. The name probably came from the nonsense, or scat, syllables that jazz musicians used to sing jazz phrases. The tempo of bop was faster, and less emphasis was placed on arrangements. Instead, it emphasized improvisation by soloists. Harmonies and melodies were more complex, and overall bop was more aggressive and hard-hitting than swing jazz was. Scatman picked it up in his travels, by listening to other musicians. He took to it naturally because he was in the habit of featuring his sidemen in solos, and because its hard-driving complexity appealed to him and his men. But, realizing that it was more difficult for audiences to understand than swing, he did not feature bop exclusively; rather, he included it in his wide repertoire.

Scatman and the band were a big hit at the various clubs in the Loop. The band was held over indefinitely at the Capitol Lounge, where he alternated with Snub Mosley. They later played at the Hollywood Show Lounge as well as at the Parisian Room at Sam Wilcox's Café de Society on the South Side.

"We were doing pretty good then," says Helen. "The band was real good. They played everything—love songs, jazz, bop, bebop. And Scat was wearing those zoot suits. He used to wear those pants way up to his chest. I'll never forget those pants as long as I live.

"It seemed so long until we finally got straight financially. It was good not to have to worry about paying the bills. I started saving. I'd put something away every week. Even if it was just ten dollars, I put it in the bank. Scat always turned the money over to me. If he needed something, he'd ask me for it."

In Chicago, they could now afford to stay at the DuSable Hotel, a fine black establishment named after Jean Baptiste Du Sable, who had built the first settlement in the area known to the Indians as "Eschikago." It was an enjoyable six months, and they experienced relatively little discrimination. But with Scatman playing mostly in white clubs, one or two incidents were inevitable.

"Once in Chicago," Helen recalls, "I think it was at the Capitol Lounge, I was sitting at the bar. The bartender didn't know I was Scat's wife, although the boss did. Some fellow was sitting next to me, talking to me and trying to make me. Then during intermission, Scat came down, and he said, 'Honey, come on in the back so we can talk.' I went back there, and when I returned to the bar after intermission, the guy and the bartender started calling me a nigger lover and all kinds of things. Scat jumped off the bandstand. He had a switchblade, and he was getting ready to use it. The boss came out and the bouncer, and they threw the guy out of the club. And then the boss turned to the bartender and said, 'And you mind your business.' "

While Scatman was in Chicago, Gervis took out the first full-page ad in which Scatman had ever been featured, and it became the basis for their scrapbook. "I started it," says Helen, "and then I think he put a few things in there, but I'm the one who really kept it up. I read all the papers and every time there was an advertisement or a review, I would cut it out and paste it in the book."

He was billed as "The Original Scat Man." "There was a black fellow who used to call himself Little Scat or something, taking after Scat, and that's why Scat started calling himself the original," says Helen.

Thanks to Gervis, Scatman got a lot of press in Chicago, all of it good. Wrote a reviewer of his Café de Society performances, " 'Scat Man' Crothers is an expert in the delineation of that particular mode of song styling, doing his highly applauded numbers from the drum-stand in the orchestra. He is a 'swing-out' music-maker along with his vocal specialties and patrons of the Café de Society are enthused over his brilliant performances."

Wrote Ted Watson of Scatman's opening engagement in Chicago at the Capitol Lounge: "Bounding into the Chicago night life and musical scene on a wave of vast popularity is Scat Man Crothers, noted eccentric drummer, whose fantastic yet real ability on the hides has been acclaimed by critics from coast to coast . . . According to reports received from the Ohio territory and Down Beat magazine, Scat Man is the latest and most outstanding 'find' in the hide business. He too masters a triple beat which is rounded out with numerous acts of clowning and jive, that certain something which tags him as a finesse king in this department."

After a successful run at the Capitol Lounge, Scatman announced that he was breaking up his band and forming a trio. Even though he was doing well, he had decided, again, that being responsible for a large band was too much trouble. With his trio, he went into Elmer's Lounge and enjoyed the new arrangement.

But soon Gervis asked Scatman if he would be interested in going out to Hollywood with a larger band. Scatman had never been to the West Coast before, and was eager to see what it was like, so he called Jimmy Harris and Duke Crowder from his earlier band, added some more sidemen to make a seven-piece band, and took off for Los Angeles.

"My father had just died," recalls Helen, "so I didn't drive out there with him. I had to go back to Ohio, and I joined him later. Scat and the boys were driving through Arkansas, I think, in the two cars. He was driving a white Cadillac and he had our dog, which was white—he called it Whitey—in the car with him. He stopped at a gas station, and he was getting ready to pull away when the guy said, 'I see you've got a white Cadillac . . . and whitewall tires . . . and a white dog. . . .'" This guy was acting like Scat had no business with anything that was white. So Scat decided to put him straight. As he pulled off, he said, 'Yeah, man, and I've got a white wife, too.' "

After her father's funeral and a visit to her family, Helen went out to Los Angeles by train. "We stopped in Texas," she says, "and they had colored rest rooms and white rest rooms, and I couldn't understand that. But I went to the white rest room, and when I came out, a black woman with a couple of children was coming out of the colored rest room. There were some benches by the rest rooms, and she sat down on one, and I sat down next to her. I started telling her how unfair I thought it was to have separate rest rooms. It really hurt me. I'm married to a black man, and here they are treating his people like that. The next thing I knew, a bunch of white men walked past me, giving me dirty looks. I don't know what they would have done if I'd stayed around there much longer, but I had to get on the train.

"Another time, I was in Kentucky visiting my brother, who was sick in the hospital. I got on the bus, and I didn't know that only black people were supposed to sit in the back. There was only one empty seat, and it was in the back, and I sat down next to this black woman and started talking to her. Everybody was looking at me. The whites looked like they wanted to grab me off that bus and kill me. But I sat there. I just sat there until the bus stopped at the hospital, and I got off."

Hollywood was no bed of roses for blacks in the 1940s either. A sizable percentage of its population were lower-class whites who had moved to California to escape the Depression Dust Bowl. Middle-and upper-class white residents of the area were not much more advanced in their racial consciousness. In the late 1940s, black stars like Nat King Cole and Lena Horne would come up against restrictive covenants when they tried to purchase homes befitting their status, and which were only available in otherwise all-white neighborhoods. Most white nightclubs refused to allow black patrons, and many were averse to booking black talent.

Helen recalls one incident that occurred shortly after they arrived. "When we were in Hollywood in 1944, Scat and the fellows wanted to take their music somewhere, I guess it was over to the club. We drove up in the car in front of this place on

Vine Street, and he went in, while I waited in the car. This sailor came by and started calling me nigger lover, and some fellow who worked with Scat in the band came out and said, 'Is he bothering you?' I said, 'I'm ignoring him.' He told the guy to go on and get lost."

But musically, Scatman believed that they had made the right move. The main theater of the war had now moved to the Pacific, and West Coast cities were filled with servicemen and their families. They needed entertaining, and a myriad of clubs had sprung up to satisfy that need. Scatman recalled, "Hollywood was jumping in those days. I was booked into the Billy Berg Swing Club, which was located at 1710 North Las Palmas. At that time there were about four clubs in that area. There was the Susie Q on the corner of Hollywood and Las Palmas, and right around the corner was the Jade Room, which specialized in Dixieland music. I can't think of the name of the other club—it was downstairs, and all the big stars used to go there."

They stayed at the Civic Hotel while Scatman played at Billy Berg's. Says Helen, "Scat had a seven-piece band, and they were really swinging."

Said Scatman, "I brought bop to Hollywood. We were playing bop when I came here with my band in '44. And when I got out here with these people, I could see how far behind they were. I said to myself, 'This is another world out here.' "

Billy Berg's Swing Club was mob-connected, as many clubs were in those days. Berg's club was also segregated, until a young white jazz buff named Norman Granz persuaded him to drop his segregated policy after Billie Holiday complained to Granz that some of her black friends could not go to the club to hear her.

Granz had worked his way through the University of California at Los Angeles by clerking at a brokerage house. While at UCLA, he had developed an interest in jazz and started collecting jazz records. A chance meeting with Nat King Cole had helped him get closer to the world of jazz musicians—a world, he discovered, upon which segregation had been rigidly imposed.

Granz told John McDonough for *Down Beat* in 1979, "Black

musicians were playing all over Los Angeles in the early '40s, but almost entirely to white audiences. This was because there were very few places that welcomed blacks as patrons. I was particularly aware of this because in addition to my day job as a film editor at MGM, I had been putting on occasional jam sessions at the Trouville Club in the Beverly Fairfax area."

Ganz approached Billy Berg with the idea of turning Sunday afternoons, when the Swing Club was ordinarily closed, into jam sessions. There would be no dancing at the sessions, only serious listening. Furthermore, not only for jam sessions, but at all times, Billy Berg's club would be open to integrated audiences. The jam sessions proved so popular that soon they were being held not just on Sunday afternoons but also on Monday nights. A new musicians' union rule guaranteeing regularly employed musicians one night off a week provided Granz with the opportunity to stage jam sessions one week night.

Scatman and Helen kept in their scrapbook a card on which Scatman wrote "First time out in Calif." The card announced his arrival as well as two jam sessions:

Get Your Kicks!
Swing Club
Announces Two Jam Sessions
Sunday Afternoon at 4—and—Monday Night at 8
Get in Early
Also Coming to Hollywood for the First Time
Opening Thursday, January 13th
The Original "Scat Man" and His Orchestra

"Yeah," said Scatman, "I played in those early jam sessions arranged by Norman Granz. This was when Hollywood was really jumpin'. This was when Frankie Laine used to come in and ask if he could sing a number. Back in '45, he told me that his record was starting to sell. I said, 'What record?' He said, ' "That's My Desire." ' So you know the rest of that."

In mid-April, while Scat Man and His Band were still performing at the Swing Club, Zutty Singleton joined the group for a time. Born in 1898 in New Orleans, Singleton was among the first to use wire brushes to strike his drums and used brushes on Louis Armstrong's 1928 recordings of "St. James Infirmary" and "Skip the Gutter." He also pioneered the use of the bass drum on all four beats of each measure. Formerly of Happy Johnson's Band, and of Nappy LaMar's Quartet, Singleton was strongly featured on drums with Scat, but he soon left to join another band.

Scatman also played at least once at the Hollywood Canteen for servicemen, and saved the March 30, 1944, thank-you letter he received from John te Groen, vice president of Local 47 of the American Federation of Musicians and chairman of the Music Committee of the Hollywood Canteen.

Also around that time, he appeared in the cast of *Insults of 1944*, starring pantomimist Ray Bourbon, at the Playtime Theater in Los Angeles. But his first stage work led to no further bookings in that area of the entertainment business.

After about six months in Hollywood, Scatman reformed his band, contacting former piano player Oliver Michaux. On trumpet were Paul Quinquette and Jimmy Lot, and Turk was again playing bass. "We had a gig in Pocatello, Idaho," Scatman recalled, "This ofay boy that played the tenor—he was about seventeen or eighteen years old—he said, 'I sure would like to go to Pocatello with you.' I said, 'But I ain't going to be able to pay you.' He said, 'If you can just pay my room and board.' He played a beautiful tenor. His name was Stan Getz."

One wouldn't expect a place like Pocatello, Idaho, to evoke fond memories for Scatman and Helen years afterward. But both would mention it frequently.

Said Scatman, "Now, Pocatello, Idaho, was a wide-open town in '44—gambling, red light district. Made a lotta money in Pocatello. I worked for a guy named Bill Hugh, who had a nightclub and gambling place, for four, five months. We stayed at a place owned by a Mr. Willard. He had some cabins and a club. I went through there a few years ago, and now he's got his own town, called Willardville. I wrote a tune about Pocatello. It went:

"Pocatella is a groovy little town
Way up in Idaho.
There is plenty of everything around
that makes you love it so.
Hey fella, if you want to get wella,
go to Pocatella.
Everyone you meet is really allreet.
It's a wonderful treat.
Pocatella is a groovy little town,
way up in Idaho."

Helen Crothers has her own warm memories of Pocatello, Idaho. "Mr. Willard had cabins, and they were so nice. His wife said, 'Instead of giving you one cabin, why don't you take two and use one for a kitchen and one for your bedroom? Or, we've got a big house up there, and if you'd prefer that, you and your husband can take that and we'll let the band stay in the cabins.' But I said, 'No, there's five fellas in the band, let them take the house.' And the next morning she came down with this big basket of homemade jams and jellies. She said, 'You take out what you want and give the rest to the boys.'

"While we were staying in those cabins, a white family— man, wife, and a little boy who must have been about six or seven years old—moved in next to us. Scat came out of the cabin one day, and the little boy said, 'Hi, nigger.' Well, I heard that, and Scat didn't even have a chance to answer. I jumped up and ran out to him, and I said, 'You little red-faced boy, you've got your nerve calling my husband a nigger.' And Mr. Willard heard me, and he came down and asked, 'What's wrong, Mrs. Crothers?' I told him, and he just said to them, 'Get your things together and get out of here in an hour.' He made them move. He was a beautiful man.

"In Pocatello, I had a cabdriver who would pick me up and take me to the club every night, and he was just as faithful. He'd come, and I'd let him stay with me until I got ready to go home.

"Those were real people in Pocatello. They were farmers, and the women wore housedresses to the club. The guys would

wear their overalls. They'd throw those silver dollars up onstage
for Scat, and he'd wind up sometimes with five or six hundred
dollars a night from them just coming up there and putting
money in the kitty or throwing it up to him. They really loved
him.

"Just before we left Pocatello, Scat had an accident. He was
driving the Cadillac and some woman ran in front of him, and
he didn't want to hit her so he hit a tree. We had to catch a train
out of town. Almost everybody—all the lady bartenders from
the club, all the gamblers, the Willards, and the taxicab driver—
was at the station to say good-bye. It was like we were a king and
queen, and that was pretty unusual in those days."

From Pocatello, they went to Newark, New Jersey, where
Scatman headlined the bill at Louis's 333 Club. An advertisement for his engagement at the club went like this:

> Wow! He's Terrific! Wotta Show! Dancing Nitely to
> The Hottest Band in Town, The Original "Scat Man"
> and His 5-Piece Orchestra. "They Sing—They Swing
> They'll Drive Your Cares Away" The "Sock" Band of
> the Year! says Billboard. Recently completing a record-
> breaking engagement at the SWING CLUB, Holly-
> wood, Calif.

From Newark, they went to Germantown, Pennsylvania,
where Scatman and his band played at a club that he recalled
"was owned by a big underworld figure." An incident at that
club was one of the few times he and Helen had trouble that
Scatman recalled vividly: "Before Helen came in, the bartender
was very friendly and everything was nice. As soon as my wife
came in, one of the customers passed a remark.

"I liked to turn the joint out. The band was playing behind
the bar, so I grabbed up a whiskey bottle and yelled, 'Let him
come on over here.' But they hustled the guy out.

"The next day I had to go down and talk to Sam. I just told
him I wasn't bothering nobody, and this guy was going to come
over the bar at me. I was just going to protect myself. I told him

that self-preservation is the first law of nature, and he agreed with me."

Scatman and the band and Helen then went back to the Midwest for several months, during which time Scatman and the band performed at the Ponthouse nightclub in Akron, Ohio, and participated in a war-loan drive there. During this time, Scatman also started composing songs. "Every one of them was for me," says Helen.

The first, "Truly I Do," he started writing in Dayton, and he kept working on it off and on. He completed the final version on January 28, 1945. The small piece of paper on which he wrote the song was one of his entries into the scrapbook.

> Dearest one, you are so dear to me
> I want you near to me
> Truly I do
> When I'm away from you
> Each night I pray for you
> Truly I do
> Life, you know, is funny
> And things aren't always sunny
> But please believe me, honey
> I do, love you
> And dearest one, I'll never lose with you
> Till now I never knew
> That truly I do
> Really love you, baby
> Truly, truly, I do.

For the next forty-odd years, he sang that song often, not only to Helen but on radio shows. In 1981, on the *Weekend L.A.* show with Sonny Melendrez on KNVC, after Melendrez asked him if he composed songs, Scat sang "Truly I Do," and was in tears as he finished it. "I'm sorry, man," he said, "every time I sing that song. . . ."

"He just cried when he sang that song," says Helen. "Wherever he was, whenever he sang it, he cried."

Sadly, that was one of the last entries in the scrapbook that Helen had so lovingly kept. "We were in Akron," she recalls. "Scat was playing at the Kit Kat Club and Harry's Black and Tan, and this man came up to our hotel room and Scat showed him the scrapbook. He asked to borrow it to show his wife, and Scat let him. The man never brought it back. I was heartsick, because I'd kept every little piece of paper, every little mention of Scat. After that, I just didn't save many reviews and articles anymore, except for a few things here and there. I did save pictures."

Later that year, 1945, they headed back to California. "We drove out to the West Coast," says Helen, "in two cars. I remember we stopped in Arkansas, and this white man saw us. We asked for a drink of water, and he charged us fifty cents apiece for a drink of water. And you know, in those days, fifty cents was like five dollars today. But he was just prejudiced because he saw a mixed couple. There was another incident when we stopped to get some gas. Our dog got out and lifted his leg up and was getting ready to pee on a bush. This white guy comes out and says, 'No, you can't do that. I won't have it.' And Scat says, 'Well, if my dog can't take a leak here, we're not buying any gas,' and we drove off."

Teddy Edwards, who plays saxophone, was working with trumpet player Howard McGee in 1945. "We were at the Swing Club on Las Palmas and Hollywood Boulevard, and Billy Berg had sent for Scat to come out. He had his own group. He had an excellent bass player named Vic Macmillan; he brought him out here from Cleveland. Vic Macmillan made some of the first West Coast records with Charlie Parker. He did 'Ornithology' and 'Dogwood Suite' and those things for Dial Records. Scatman also had the great trumpet player Benny Bailey, one of the finest trumpet players in the world today. The piano player was named Tommy. He had excellent musicians.

"Scatman was playing the stand-up cocktail drums, like a built-up tom-tom with cymbals and things on it. He played that and did his singing and his comedy routines, which were very, very clever. My dear friend Spanky Wilson, the vocalist, was doing this takeoff on 'Pennies From Heaven,' and her first knowledge of it was an Eddie Jefferson recording of it. I said to her, 'Darlin', I heard Scatman do that in 1945.'

"Scatman told this story about this soldier who goes overseas, and he comes back and his wife got a baby named Benny. He wants to know where Benny came from, and she told him Benny was from heaven.

"He did a takeoff on 'South of the Border'—you know, 'South of the border, down Mexico way,' only in his version it was 'South of the border . . . in a Mexican way.'

"He did another one where he imitated a lighthouse. He'd turn around in a circle, and when he'd face the audience, he'd open his mouth and close it. He was very clever."

"He did a thing about baseball, a very funny routine. He would act like he was a homosexual at the ball game. Goosey was the batter, and when he hit a long ball, Scat would say, 'Smash it, Goosey, smash it, honey.' The umpire would say, 'Three balls and one strike.' and Scat would say, '*Three* balls???' The announcer would say, 'He knocked up a fly,' and Scat would say, 'Knocked up a fly???' He was really funny, and it wasn't offensive or derogatory to anyone."

In late 1945, Scatman and his band went north for an engagement at the Back Stage Bar in San Francisco. There, Helen recalls, they encountered more prejudice.

"We had paid for a week in one place in San Francisco, but when they found out we had a dog, they said no, no dogs. The room had linoleum on the floor! Now what could a dog do to linoleum? I always carried newspapers and plastic to put underneath him. Anyway, our dog was trained. He would bark and let you know if he wanted to go out. We could put him on the elevator of a hotel, and when he got to the ground floor, he'd bark, and they'd let him out, and he'd do his business, and come back in, and they'd put him back on the elevator, and he'd come back up. But they didn't want us because of the dog. I never did believe that. I told Scat they just didn't want us because we were mixed. But Scat said, 'All right, thank you,' and we walked out. We would always wind up staying with the black people in those days—rooming houses, apartments."

"Sometimes it *was* because of the dog that we couldn't stay certain places. Although we were often the first mixed couple to check into certain hotels, most of the places we were turned down was because of the dog."

They were in San Francisco about six weeks. Coincidentally, the Howard McGee group was playing at the Back Stage Bar at the same time, so Teddy Edwards and Scatman continued their friendship. Edwards recalls that it was while he was in San Francisco that he first began to realize the effect the end of the war would have on the music business.

"My father wrote me a letter saying. 'Get out of California because the war's winding down, and California's never been kind to artists.' And he was so right. When we got back here, the bottom had dropped out. We were up in San Francisco for six weeks, and by the time we got back to Los Angeles, it was a different city. Los Angeles had been a twenty-four-hour city. Central Avenue had been jumping all night long, and everywhere it was just swinging. We got back, and all that had changed."

The soldiers and their girlfriends and families were moving back home. The clubs were empty, and soon many closed down. There was little work for musicians. "The servicemen didn't have that money to throw away anymore," says Edwards. "And all those war jobs that the women had because the men were at war—all those went down the drain. We were just scratching. Howard [McGee] didn't have a group except sparingly; we played here and there now and then. That's when Scatman disbanded his group, more or less. It was three or four years before we recovered."

Still, Scatman and Helen decided to stay in Los Angeles and make it their home base. "We stayed at a black hotel, the Civic Hotel, on First and San Pedro," Helen recalls. "We stayed there for quite a while."

Like the Howard McGee group, Scatman and his musicians got work here and there. Scatman also performed as a single when he could. He performed occasionally at San Quentin State Prison, including one time in early December 1945. Evidently, he heard at least one hard-luck story there, for in his December 10, 1945, letter thanking Scatman, warden Clinton Duffy wrote, "I have had deposited to the inmate's account you specified, the $5 left with me."

"Scat helped people all the time," says Helen.

In 1946, Helen went back home to visit her family, occasioning Scatman to write another song, "Waiting for My Baby." He explained, "She went back to Steubenville, Ohio, to visit her folks. She was only gone five or six weeks, but, man, it seemed like years." The following is one verse from the song:

> Oh, she's adorable, lovable and charmin' too
> Dependable, reliable, al-wayyyyys true
> It's oh so plain to seeeeee, baby
> You're the one for meeeee
> And I'm waiting for my baby to come back

By the summer of 1946, bookings for Scatman with or without his band were so scarce, he accepted an offer from Slim Gaillard, an eccentric guitarist, to join the Slim Gaillard Trio as drummer.

Gaillard was popular enough to weather the hard times. He had written "Flat Foot Floosie" and "Cement Mixer," two novelty hits, and was a "hipster" par excellence, a master of hip lingo. Among his favorite expressions were: Mac-voutie, mellowroonie, scootlier-reeti, and groovey-ovoutie. His stage performance was similar in feeling—he hopped from the piano to the steel guitar and back again, displaying incredible energy.

The advantage of playing with Gaillard for Scatman was that he was paid good money and had the opportunity to play in the big theaters downtown. With Gaillard, Scatman got his first opportunity to appear at Los Angeles's big Orpheum Theater on a star-studded bill that included Jimmie Lunceford and his orchestra and Ivie Anderson, the singer who had become famous with Duke Ellington's orchestra, for one stint, drummer Buddy Rich for another. But the name Scat Man Crothers was not on the bill. He was merely a member of the Slim Gaillard Trio.

By all accounts, the music the trio played was right up Scat-man's alley. Wrote the reviewer for the Gaillard Trio/Buddy Rich show, "Just what the trio plays, I don't know, and I'll bet even they couldn't repeat it five minutes later. They use some wonderful satirical touches in their work, but their large following seems only interested in the rhythm they dish out.

"They're an o-voutie, o-rooney, o-reeny of a team and when they join the Rich organization for the finale, they achieve the ultimate in jive."

But Helen Crothers says Scatman did not enjoy working with the Slim Gaillard Trio. "He was used to having a band, you know, and playing by himself. And Slim Gaillard didn't want to show anybody else's talent. He just wanted Scat to play drums. He knew Scat could sing, but he wouldn't let him, except when it was all three of them singing. Scat would say to me, 'He's different than I am [as a bandleader]. I want my men to sing, to do whatever they do, and show what kind of talent they have.' He didn't stay with Slim Gaillard very long, maybe five or six months. Slim Gaillard was well known for a while, but then I don't know what happened to him."

Scatman went out as a single again, making the rounds of the Hollywood clubs, including the Cricket Club on West Washington at Vermont, where he appeared with Vic Dickinson and His Orchestra. In 1948, he was working at the Oasis, a white club. "It was a beautiful club," he said. "Carol Burnett's ex-husband was going to USC then. I bought him many a drink. It was 1948, when they didn't want any blacks in the club. I told the owner, 'If you want to make some money, what you should do is turn this club into a black and tan. I've got just the man for you to meet.' I introduced him to Curtis Mosely, a club operator I knew, and together they turned the club into a black and tan and that's when they started making money. That's the same advice I gave to the owner of the Chesame back in Dayton, Ohio, and he took it, too."

During that time, Scatman was introduced to musician and radio star Phil Harris by Eddie "Rochester" Anderson, both of whom were regulars on Jack Benny's radio program, and both of whom were musicians who liked to hang out at the jazz clubs.

"He was one of the hardest workers I've ever seen, and he started practically working out on the street in Los Angeles," says Harris. "He played every slop jar in town, if you know what I mean. He played a little thing that was like what we called a tipple, between a ukulele and a guitar, and he had it tuned like a ukulele.

"I used to see him a lot out on Vine Street. I saw a lot of guys start out on Vine Street, in the Famous Door, Billy Berg's, the basement of the hotel on Hollywood Boulevard, and other places where everybody used to get together and jam. There was never any color line between black and white musicians. We loved to get together with the black musicians—they had so much talent, and they were playing the kind of music that we liked. There was no animosity or jealousy. I remember Nat King Cole. We had the worst trouble getting him to sing. He didn't want to sing. He had his little trio and he was a hell of a piano player and he was very popular even then."

Harris was from Linton, Indiana, so as fellow Hoosiers he and Scatman immediately had something in common. But Harris had a steady income, while Scatman did not. "He was by himself, and he worked like a dog," says Harris, "He was doing scat songs and playing that little guitar of his, and he was very clever with it. He always had a big smile and was always laughing, always laughing. He loved jokes, and everybody took to Scatman, everybody liked him. He never took advantage of anybody, he never tried to force himself on anybody. They came to him. He was really hustling. But I never in my life saw him put the lug on anybody for a nickel."

When Harris was ten years old, his family had moved to Nashville, Tennessee, and he had friends in the music business there. He mentioned that he knew Scatman, and a few weeks later one of his friends, who worked at the local radio station, called him to say he'd written a song called "Chattanooga Shoe Shine Boy" and that he wanted Harris and Scatman to record it. They did so in 1948 for RCA-Victor.

"At that time, people were just recording singles—the LP

hadn't been invented yet," says Harris. "This guy said he thought
the record would really play. Well, we made the record, and
Scatman made a little bread and I made a few crumbs."

Scatman, who had shined many a shoe in his Terre Haute
days, provided the sound effects, popping the rag just as he had
done to earn big tips in the old days. They introduced the song
on Harris's radio show on NBC. "It was called *The Phil Harris–
Alice Faye Show*," says Harris. "We were on for seven years. I was
on with [Jack] Benny for eighteen years, and then I did seven
years of my own show, and I was still on with Jack until he went
to television."

Reviews of Scatman's appearance on the Phil Harris show
were laudatory. Wrote one reviewer, " 'Scatman's' material is
new and refreshingly different from other comics around today.
He seldom resorts to risque songs to put his act across. Some of
his numbers will make the ladies in the audience blush, but not
a deep red. Just a minor hue . . .

"An interview with 'Scatman' is as hilarious as a Bob Hope
broadcast. He jumps all over the place, never sitting still for even
a minute. The guy has more energy than a vitamin pill and, as
he puts it, 'Wind I ain't never used yet!' He's a tireless performer, singing and strumming his ukulele for as long as the
customer applauds. During one of the shows caught by this reviewer, the 'Scatman' stayed on the floor for nearly an hour. The
guys and gals in the audience kept yelling and clamoring for
more.

"His act is smooth and Big Time. . . . Among his many talents is his ability to write original songs, which he does regularly."

Two interesting aspects of this review are that nowhere in it
is Scatman identified as a Negro or colored, and that his nickname is spelled as one word.

The popularity of "Chattanooga Shoeshine Boy" and Scatman's appearance on the Phil Harris show brought increased
club bookings as well as his first opportunity to record by himself
for a major label. This chance came about by a stroke of luck.
Some years earlier, a jazz songwriter named Riff Charles had

written four songs and saved up the money to record them on his own. He asked Scatman to do the vocals and then sold the masters to Capitol Records. Capitol then signed Scatman to a contract. His first record for Capitol, in 1948, was a single, with "Dead Man's Blues" on one side and "The Thing" on the other. It retailed for seventy-nine cents. Wrote Gilbert Kean in *The Saturday Review*, "Two fine, commercial blues by Capitol's new-comer, a Pacific Coast character who, it is said, has a vogue in that sector. The Scat Man sings with an amazing coarse huski-ness, as if he had just swallowed a trombone mute. Nevertheless, the chanting is good humorous entertainment, certainly one of the provinces of music."

"Dead Man's Blues" became a classic. "You'll pay twenty-five dollars for it now," Scatman said in 1980.

Not long after "Dead Man's Blues" was released, Scatman had an offer to play at the New Orleans Swing Club in San Francisco, headlining with the Hunter Gray Trio and billed as "The Great Scatman, Broadcast and Recording Star Comedian." Helen accompanied him there, for the engagement lasted about two months. While they were in San Francisco, Helen learned that she was pregnant.

CHAPTER 5

SETTLED DOWN IN TINSEL TOWN

SCATMAN AND HELEN HAD BEEN TRYING TO HAVE A CHILD ever since they got married, but they'd been unsuccessful. "A doctor told me I had a child's womb," says Helen. "He said, 'When it develops, you'll get pregnant.'" But it had been about twelve years, and after a while I had just accepted that we would not have children. When I realized something was growing inside me, I thought I had a tumor. I went to this German doctor in San Francisco, and he said, 'You got a tumor all right, you got a baby inside you.' I was tickled to death."

When they returned to Los Angeles from San Francisco, Helen found a room on the east side of the city off of Maple in a home owned by a black woman named Mrs. Newman. But as the pregnancy progressed, Helen decided they needed an apartment. "Mrs. Newman had an apartment over on Hobart off Pico, and we rented that," says Helen. "I bought a big baby bed

like all the stars were buying. You could convert it into a small
bed and a child could sleep in it until eight years old. And I
bought all sorts of baby clothes."

Meanwhile, Scatman took every job he could find, aware
that he would soon have another mouth to feed. "In 1949 I
worked the Bingo Club, which is now the Sahara [in Las Vegas],"
he recalled. "I had a four-week contract. So I went in through
the front door a couple of times, and the guy came up to me and
said, 'You're not supposed to come in the front door.' I said,
'What'd you say?' He repeated it, and I said, 'Look, man, I used
the front door just like everybody else.' And I did. So they cut
me from four weeks to two weeks, but I still walked in that front
door. They thought I was crazy, but hell, I wasn't working in the
kitchen."

About a month before Helen was due to give birth, she had
an X ray. "It showed that the baby was in the perfect position to
come out," says Helen. All other indications were that she would
carry the baby to term, so Scatman continued to accept jobs out
of the city.

Around that time, Scatman went back to San Francisco,
where he worked on Eddie King's radio show and played several
club dates. As the March due date for the baby approached, he
decided he wanted to be with his wife, so he drove back to Los
Angeles.

"He got home about four o'clock in the morning," says
Helen. "He was so tired, and he went to sleep. About five-thirty
that morning, my water burst. I decided not to disturb him. I
had all my things packed, and the baby clothes to take the baby
home in. I called a cab. It was very cold, and I had a big fur coat
that I had brought from back East. The cabdriver took one look
at me and said, 'Jesus!' He thought I was going to have the baby
right there. He kept looking back at me to see if anything was
happening.

"He drove me to the hospital, they used to call it Culver City
Hospital, on Hughes Avenue; now it's Brotman Memorial. I
arrived around six or six-thirty, and I stayed in that maternity
ward all day. Women kept coming in and then going to the

delivery room, and I just kept lying in that maternity ward, screaming and hollering in pain. The doctors couldn't understand what was wrong, because the X ray had been perfect. All the next day, I went through that pain. They were shooting me with pain killer because I was screaming. Finally, about nine-thirty the next morning, I screamed, 'Get my doctor.' I wanted him to do something.

"Finally, he and a surgeon delivered her. I didn't have a cesarean, but they had to cut me in order to get her out. Her head was twisted and wouldn't come down through the birth canal. But anyway, I had her, and she was a perfect little baby girl. I wanted Scat to see her, but I knew better.

"I had looked around that hospital. The only black person you saw was the man who mopped the floors. There were no black doctors, black nurses, black aides, not even any black candy stripers. And I don't think there were any black patients. I was afraid they would do something to Donna or me if they found out her father was black.

"So I called Scat and told him not to come to the hospital. It broke my heart when I'd see the other fathers standing at their wives' bedsides and looking at their babies. But I wasn't taking any chances. So I said, 'You just stay home.' "

He sent me roses every day, candy, flowers, love notes, called me several times a day. But he never did come to that hospital until Donna and I were discharged.

"Donna was kind of reddish-beige, a little bit darker than the other babies. The nurses and the other mothers suspected that I had a black man. They looked at me like I was crazy. When a nurse would bring Donna in to me, the other mothers would just be looking, and looking at each other. I just ignored them.

"But when I thought they were deliberately hurting her, I didn't ignore that. I remember they put a little bead necklace on her, and I think they deliberately put it on too tight, because her face was red, and it looked like she was choking. I said, 'My God, what are you trying to do, kill her?' and I took a pair of scissors and cut those beads off of her. And that scared me all the more.

"One nurse there was really prejudiced. The window near

my bed was broken, and the flies were coming in and getting all over my water pitcher. I asked her for some fresh water, but she just ignored me and put her nose up and went and got water for other people. So I started crying, because I was really sentimental and young. And my doctor came by and asked why I was crying, and I told him what happened. He said to her, 'Nurse, are you assigned to any one patient in this ward?' She said she wasn't. He said, 'Well, go and get my patient a clean pitcher and fresh water.' She flew out of there. We still have that doctor.

"When I got ready to go home, I said to Scat, 'You come and pick me up and let them see, and I don't give a damn.' He came and there were looks—not dirty looks, just what's-going-on-here kinds of looks. I was so glad to get home.

"At home, everybody was so nice. All the neighbors came to see her, brought me little things. All black people."

Soon after Helen came home with Donna, Scatman had to go out of town again. Meanwhile, Helen had decided they needed a larger apartment. Her brother was visiting, and he helped her move to a spacious upstairs flat in a house on Saturn off West Boulevard owned by a Mrs. Corbin. After about nine months there, they decided to move again. It took several moves to convince them that it was time for something more permanent.

"Scat and I said to each other, 'We need to settle down and get a house.' And we bought a house on Thirty-eighth and Cimmaron—1877 West Thirty-eighth Street. When we moved in there, Donna was two and a half. We had cement poured in the back, and we had her little hand and footprints put in there.

"It was a great big house. We had two nice-sized bedrooms, a huge living room and dining room combination, a huge kitchen, a big service porch, a huge backyard. We had a big front yard with grass on both sides. We lived on a corner, and our lot was a whole half a block.

"When we first moved in there, we went to sleep many a night with our door open. I used to leave Donna's tricycle, her little swimming pool, all of her toys, out in front. Nobody touched anything. It changed a lot in the twenty-one years we lived there."

The house was a wonderful place to raise Donna, but it was a major added responsibility for Scatman, who had to work even harder to pay for it. There were times when they could barely make or fell behind on the mortgage payments. Scatman never despaired, however. Characteristically, he joked about the vagaries of his career: "They shoulda called me yo-yo, I was uppin' and downin' so often."

Scatman was still performing out of town a lot, especially in San Francisco and Sacramento. Helen rarely went with him. "Donna was too small," she says, "and I didn't want to leave her with anybody. I didn't miss the traveling. He worked in Lake Tahoe for quite a while, a few months, and he would call every night, and once in a while, on his day off, he would come home for a visit."

When Donna was older, Helen would sometimes join him on weekends. "I would leave Donna with a lady named Molly, a Jewish woman, who used to take care of her and the house and the dog." She enjoyed settling down and being a housewife.

The same year Donna was born, Scatman got a big break when he began a stint on *Dixie Showboat,* a local one-hour show filmed by Paramount at the KTLA-TV studios and the first TV show to feature blacks. "It was just like *The Love Boat,* only it didn't sail," says Helen. "It was a mixed show with black and white, a variety show. Millie Bruce was the girl who worked with Scatman. She was Eddie 'Rochester' Anderson's wife's sister, and she later married Sugar Ray Robinson. Scatman and Millie were always getting engaged to be married, but they never got married. They danced a little bit and sang a little bit. There was a blackface comedy team on the show called Peanuts and Popcorn, and there was Nappy Lamar's Dixieland band. Dick Lane was the captain on the ship; he's passed away now. The show was really good, and it lasted quite a while." Scatman, who was paid twenty-five dollars a week, was a regular on the show from 1948 to 1951.

"It was on Channel Five," he recalled. "Every week we would be on a different levee. The set was nothing but bales of cotton. People would come and sit on the bales of cotton and do their numbers. My last number on every show was with Millie Bruce. As a matter of fact, she was so pretty I wrote a tune about Millie called 'The Gal Looks Good.'

> "I got a gal I know ain't true
> Her boyfriends number quite a few
> I should quit. What can I do?
> The gal looks *good*."

"That was when television was in its infancy," Scatman recalled. "We were in kinescope. We only had one camera, so there was a lot of panning because it was always on. And anything that went wrong, from actors fluffing their lines to sets falling down in mid-scene, you let it go by. Just keep on going or else the whole show wouldn't be on the air."

Scatman was a natural for the new medium. Not only did he have a lively manner and great musical talent, but his face was quintessentially expressive. In those days with just one camera and no close-ups, his oversized facial features seemed to fill the TV screen, and his incandescent smile seemed to augment the primitive lighting system of the studio.

Around 1950, he also started getting exposure on local TV and radio shows hosted by Larry Finley. "I had a restaurant on the Sunset Strip, and I did a radio interview show from the restaurant," says Finley. "It was on KFWB, and it was called *Larry Finley's My Own Place,* and it was the number-one-rated show in town at the time. All the press agents and the promotional people used to come around and try to get their people on. But the way I first met Scat was when he walked in cold one night, and I put him on. I'd never heard of him before. He didn't perform, he didn't sing. We just chatted, and I took a liking to him.

"At the time, he was appearing at some black nightclub in Los Angeles. That's what we talked about when he got on the air—his appearance at that club. I went to the club and caught his act a couple of days later.

"This was around 1950. Later, I also had a TV show on

KNXT, Channel Two, called *Strictly Informal,* and that's when I first exposed Scatman on television.

"There was a great deal of racism in California at that time, and there was resistance to blacks appearing on television. A couple of years later, the *Los Angeles Examiner* was my sponsor on a show on ABC called *Music Is My Beat,* and I used to have Scat and Nat King Cole on all the time. I also had Pearl Bailey on, and I put my arms around her. And then there was Sammy Davis, Jr. I remember the *Examiner* got a lot of letters calling me a nigger lover, and some people canceled their subscriptions in protest. But I didn't care. Every time I had Scat on my show, we embraced each other, and he called me his Jewish Brother, and I called him my Black Brother, and we did that on the air all the time.

"Of course, we didn't pay much. The AFTRA Guild-mandated pay was something like twenty-six dollars for a half-hour show, but at that time twenty-six bucks meant an awful lot to Scat. That, and the exposure."

Scatman's appearances on Finley's shows and his work on *Dixie Showboat* led to his being considered for the role of Lightnin' on the soon-to-be televised *Amos 'n' Andy* show, a role that eventually went to Nick Stewart. Scatman did appear in a guest slot on one of the shows, the first televised black sitcom.

The early 1950s saw a change in television programming that reflected the new political consciousness of black Americans and a new national temperament that was more responsive to black concerns, despite the considerable racism in California and elsewhere. With good reason, blacks understood that image was important, especially on television, which was fast becoming a fixture in American homes. If there were no blacks on television, then the implication was that they were invisible in American life. Blacks did not like that implication, and the networks started to address their concern.

Understandably, with black sitcoms being uncharted territory, the networks first looked to successful radio shows with black characters. *Amos 'n' Andy* had been a popular radio show since its early days as a local show out of Chicago in 1926. Picked

up and run nationally by NBC in 1929, it was a fifteen-minute
show that ran for six nights a week until 1943, when it became
a half-hour show. During all those years, the roles were played
by whites. In 1948, CBS decided to bring it to television, this
time with black actors. It lasted two years, from 1951 to 1953.

Beulah predated *Amos 'n' Andy* on television by one year,
running from October 1950 to September 1953. Also formerly
a popular radio series, *Beulah* had been a spin-off from *The
Fibber McGee and Molly Show*. Played by a white actor named
Marlin Hunt, Beulah proved to be such a popular character that
the *Beulah* radio series was developed in 1945. Hunt originated
that role but was later replaced by another white actor, Bob
Corley. Finally, in 1947, Hattie McDaniel, most famous for her
1939 portrayal of Mammy in *Gone With the Wind,* became the
first black woman to play the role. She was taken into American
hearts as the feisty maid to the white Henderson family, and
when ABC made plans to bring the show to television, she was the
first choice to play the character. McDaniel soon fell ill, however,
and Ethel Waters took over the part. Scatman appeared as a guest
star in the first fifteen shows, as a friend of Bill, the chauffeur.

His only steady work on television was in cartoons, and
while it brought him a regular paycheck, it gave no exposure to
anything but his voice. One of the first blacks to do voices on
television, he did the voices for two characters on the TV puppet
adventure *Time for Beany,* a fifteen-minute syndicated show that
premiered in 1949 and was the first children's show to win an
Emmy award.

Based on characters created by Bob Clampett, the show was
about the misadventures of a small boy named Beany, his pet sea
serpent, Cecil, and Horatio K. Huffenpuff, the captain of a boat
called the *Leakin' Lena.* There were several other characters,
including the Wildman and Go Man Gogh, for which Scatman
provided the voices. Humorist Stan Freberg, Daws Butler, and
Harry Colonna did the rest of the voices.

Scatman's biggest television break in the 1950s was being
invited to appear on *The Colgate Comedy Hour* with the young
comedian Donald O'Connor, who served as host on the show

between 1951 and 1954. Scatman first appeared on the show in 1951, and became a regular the following year in a role created just for him that was described as a "be-bop characterization" in the magazine *The Baton,* which went on to describe Scatman as "A born funny man, his exaggerated loose-limbed movements in a small compact body, ad-libbed patter, dancing feet, and, in recent years, his sleek toupee, have put him over."

Scatman had started wearing a toupee in the early 1950s. "His hair was receding even when I met him, when he was twenty-six," says Helen. "He was getting bald on top, and so he went into this place called Curvette's or something and he paid about five hundred dollars for one toupee, and in those days that was pretty high. He just started wearing it. Over the years, he must have had three or four wigs. I'd give the old ones to the Salvation Army. One time in the 1960s he came home wearing a natural [Afro] wig, and I laughed and laughed. Later on, when he got on *Chico and the Man,* he just shaved his head clean. He'd say, 'There's Kojack, and I'm Black Jack.' "

The Colgate Comedy Hour was a live show. So popular did it become that it even played Las Vegas for six weeks. Scatman did not like the idea of facing racial discrimination in Las Vegas again, but he endured it for the sake of the show. His work on *The Colgate Comedy Hour,* on which he appeared for two-and-a-half years, led to invitations to appear on *The Jack Benny Show* and *The Steve Allen Show* as well as more club bookings.

Years later he particularly remembered a booking in Kansas City in 1954. "I was with Olsen and Johnson, and I was staying at the Latin Hotel. They had these little Negro girls running the elevators, and I got on and the girl said, 'You live here?' and I said, 'Yeah.' She said, 'You're kidding.' I said, 'Okay, take me to my room. I'll prove it.' I think I was the first black dude that ever stayed in the Latin Hotel."

His exposure on *The Colgate Comedy Hour* may also have been instrumental in getting him his first job in motion pictures—performing in a fifty-four minute effort by Ron Ormond (Spartan) Productions, released in 1951 by Lippert Pic-

tures as a supporting booking in small theaters. *Yes Sir, Mr. Bones*
was a minstrel show in the old style with six songs, lots of buck-
and-wing and softshoe dancing, complete with interlocutor.
Scatman, who is listed in some sources as Scatman "Carothers,"
was one of a number of entertainers who appeared in the film.
The following year, he appeared in a similarly modest musical
film titled *Return of Gilbert and Sullivan*.

Scatman's work on *Time for Beany* and in the musical films
no doubt helped his career, or at least augmented his income.
But it is likely, again, that it was his work on *The Colgate Comedy
Hour* that also led to what he later called his really big break—his
first feature role in a Hollywood film.

"He was working at the Oasis in Los Angeles at the time,"
says Helen, "and one night Dan Dailey walked in. He called Scat
over and said, 'Scat, I'm getting ready to start work on a picture
called *Meet Me at the Fair*, and there's a part in it that's made for
you. I'm gonna write down Albert J. Cohen's name, and you go
out to Universal Studios tomorrow and talk to him. He knows
that I'm here talking to you about it because we discussed it.'
And the next day Scat went out to Universal and was hired right
on the spot. That was really a big break for him, and for us
because the money was good."

"Now, acting was the furthest thing from Scat's mind. He
was so wrapped up in his music—the band and his singing, and
his drums and his guitar. But he was a natural. He never had a
lesson in his life, never had any coaching. He has a memory like
an elephant, and he just remembered all his lines."

Given that Scatman had a dramatic role that ran through
the entire picture and appeared in 104 of the film's 208 scenes,
he had to be a "natural" to carry it off.

While sustaining dramatic roles like that of Enoch in *Meet
Me at the Fair* required a great deal of time and energy, there
were advantages. As he said during the filming, "I'm not sleeping so well, but, man, I'm eating high on the hog!"

The film was a warm, lightweight piece aimed at the family
audience and released for Christmas 1952. Eighty-seven minutes long, it was a screen adaptation by Irving Wallace of Gene

Markey's novel *The Great Companions*. Set in 1904, it starred Dan Dailey as Doc Tilbey, an itinerant patent-medicine salesman whose wonder tonic is made of alcohol and prune juice, and Scatman as his sidekick, Enoch. While playing in a small midwestern town, they pick up an eleven-year-old boy who has run away with his dog from a grim orphanage. The boy was played by Chet Allen, who attended the Columbus Boychoir of Princeton, New Jersey, and had a pleasing soprano voice.

It happens to be an election year in the town, and the crooked D.A., played by Hugh O'Brian, is afraid that word will get out about the deplorable conditions in the orphan home and that corrupt local politicos have been misappropriating orphange funds. Tilbey and Enoch find themselves charged with kidnapping, but they refuse to knuckle under. Before the film is over, they have rescued eleven more boys, and the prim social worker, played by Diana Lynn, has seen through her fiancé, the crooked D.A., and fallen in love with Dailey. In the end, the heroes have brought about much-needed reforms at the orphanage and helped to oust the crooked politicians from office.

The film was relatively light on plot and heavy on musical numbers, which suited Scatman fine. He sang or played six tunes, including "Ezekiel Saw De Wheel,' a duet with Allen called "All God's Chillun Got Wings," and another song with Allen and Dailey titled "I Was There," which Scatman co-wrote with F. E. Miller. His biggest number was "I Got the Shiniest Mouth in Town" by Stan Freberg, Scatman's "co-star voice" on *Time for Beany*.

The role of Enoch was the most important one for a Negro actor to come along in several years, and Universal International passed over a number of veteran black Hollywood actors, among them Stepin Fetchit, in favor of Scatman. Moreover, Scatman was the first black to receive such high billing in an interracial film—Scatman liked to say he was billed third, although in some sources he is given fourth billing, behind the young Chet Allen.

While there were elements of the "darky" in the role of Enoch, despite concerted efforts by the National Association for the Advancement of Colored People (NAACP) to get Holly-

wood studios to abandon such stereotypes, by the standards of
the time, Scatman's role was comparatively dignified. He was not
just Dailey's helper, but also his friend. His was not a bit part,
easily excised by southern censors, and for that reason *Meet Me
at the Fair* was shown in few Deep South venues. It was a sustaining, dramatic role, important to the story, and Scatman received critical praise for his efforts:

"Crothers does very well as Dailey's helper, easily handling
both comedy and song chores."

". . . a likeable entertainer who socks a song over with an
engaging, toothsome grin and a wonderful sense of rhythm . . .
Crothers drew a round of applause from the preview audience
with his sock delivery of 'I Got the Shiniest Mouth in Town.' "

". . . Crothers, a genial comedian, pleases as Dailey's helper."

"Scat Man Crothers, who does the funniest number in the
film, a big hit called 'Shiniest Mouth in Town.' "

" 'Scat Man Crothers has a big role as aide to the traveling
show and he draws sympathy with his portrayal."

"Crothers is a pleasing Negro comic scoring a success as
Dailey's helper with such songs as 'Ezekial Saw De Wheel' and 'I
Got the Shiniest Mouth in Town.' "

". . . Scat Man Crothers . . . has been knocking around local
nightclubs for quite some time. Fortunately, someone discovered he had talent. . . . I don't think either the Scat Man or
young [Chet] Allen will have to worry about work around the
studios."

That last reviewer's comment was prophetic, at least where
Scatman was concerned. *Meet Me at the Fair* was not yet in release
when Scatman was signed by Will Cowen, producer of musical
shorts for Universal International, for a musical featurette, *The
Nat King Cole Story,* starring Cole.

In 1953, he appeared in Universal's *East of Sumatra,* an adaptation of a story by Louis L'Amour starring Jeff Chandler as
the chief engineer of a tin-mining firm working the island of
Tunga. Scatman played Baltimore, one of Chandler's chief
aides. He played his ukulele and sang two songs he wrote especially for the film, "Strange Land" and "Ballad to a Gypsy."

Other feature roles included two more films for Universal International. In *Walking My Baby Back Home* (also 1953) starring Donald O'Connor and Janet Leigh, he played Smiley, the pianist in O'Connor's orchestra who gives O'Connor the great idea of playing symphonic Dixieland. In *Johnny Dark* (1954), starring Tony Curtis and Piper Laurie, Scatman played himself and did a couple of songs.

While none of these later roles approached the importance of that of Enoch in *Meet Me at the Fair,* Scatman was pleased with whatever film work he was offered. In his early forties by this time, Scatman had a perspective that younger actors lacked. "Hugh O'Brien had a bit part," said Scatman of *Meet Me at the Fair.* "He thought he wasn't going anywhere. I said, 'You guys are young. You don't want to quit now.' They were grooming guys like O'Brien, Tony Curtis, Rock Hudson, Stuart Whitman. Stu Whitman started to quit, and I said, 'Don't give it up now. You'll be a big star.' "

Those younger, white actors kept getting more work, and eventually did achieve stardom in films. But for Scatman, after the early burst of film work in the 1950s, there were few offers for a number of years. Partly, this lack of work may be explained by poor representation; the agents he hired did not have the clout to open the necessary doors.

But more likely, the fallow period in Scatman's film career, which, with only a few exceptions, lasted some fifteen years, was due to changes in Hollywood's attitude toward blacks, and the new image of blacks it chose to portray.

Since the early 1940s, the NAACP, particularly its executive director, Walter White, had campaigned ambitiously against traditional black stereotypes in films. Stars of an earlier era, like Hattie McDaniel, drew fire from the NAACP for speaking in dialect and for playing servant roles. By the middle 1940s, the NAACP's campaign had resulted in an unintended result—the major studios had all but ceased to use blacks in any roles at all. Unemployment among black screenplayers reached unprecedented rates, and in September 1946 the predominantly white Screen Actors Guild came out against the "silent boycott" of black actors by both major and independent studios. A resolution was adopted that called upon SAG to use all its power to oppose discrimination against blacks in the motion-picture industry and called for the establishment of a special committee to meet with representatives of other entertainment guilds to "establish in the industry a policy of presenting Negro characters on the screen in the true relation they bear to American life."

Mindful of the racism in the country, especially in the South, the studios were still loath to present blacks as equal to whites. The role of Enoch in *Meet Me at the Fair* was thus an anomaly. Only later in the decade did the studios settle on a proper new image for blacks, and unfortunately it was an image that left Scatman out.

It was an image personified by Sidney Poitier—intelligent, upright, dignified. No singing, no dancing, no clowning. The female image was best represented by Dorothy Dandridge, the archetypal tragic mulatto.

Scatman had a bit part in *Between Heaven and Hell* (20th Century–Fox, 1956), starring Robert Wagner, and a part in the 1958 film *The Gift of Love* (also for 20th Century–Fox), although he wasn't even listed in the credits. The money he earned from these roles was not enough to pay the mortgage.

He continued to record, doing two songs of his own composition for Capitol, "I'd Rather Be a Humming Bird" and "Blue-Eyed Sally," and four songs for the London label— "Television Blues," "I'd Rather Be a Rooster (With a Flock of Chicks)," "The Whale Song," and "The Atom Bomb Blues."

Two other songs he recorded in the fifties were substantial hits. One was "Walkin' My Baby Back Home," from the film in which he had appeared with Donald O'Connor and Janet Leigh. The other was "On the Sunny Side of the Street." Recorded for Decca, it was Scatman's biggest-selling record, and would be associated with him for years afterward.

Thanks to these hits, Scatman was invited to appear on musical variety television shows, which pleased him. Despite the fact that he had written "Television Blues," lamenting the negative impact of television on live musical performance, he believed "Television offers the best opportunity for young people and for Negroes. We have to be seen in order to be enjoyed."

Music and performing it remained Scatman's first love, and he continued to appear regularly in nightclubs, primarily white clubs in the Los Angeles area. Around the time he appeared on the Phil Harris radio show, he was at Maury Glick's Melody Club. Occasionally, he ranged farther afield, performing with Vivian Green and the Fine Scamps at the Rossonian Lounge in Denver, Colorado.

He was also invited back to Las Vegas. "He got a job at the Riviera," says Helen. "We couldn't live at the hotel, so we had to stay over where the black people lived on the other side of town. Everyone called it Dustville. I would go to the hotel as a customer, but I wouldn't let anybody know I was Scatman's wife; I didn't want to jeopardize his job. But after I'd had a few drinks, I'd have to leave, because I'd be smiling at him and throwing kisses at him and saying, 'He's my husband.' "

"I remember seeing this nice-looking black marine come in, and he stood at the bar, and the bartender waited on everybody but him. I said to myself, 'Isn't this terrible?' and I wanted to say something, but I was afraid I'd start a riot."

"In later years, when we went there, they treated us like the king and queen. Barron Hilton gave us the presidential suite when Scat and I went there for some charity for disabled athletes in the early 1980s. We had seven keys to the suite, because we had one whole corner of a floor with five doors, three huge bedrooms, three baths, a Jacuzzi, three wet bars, a huge dining room. It was so big you could get lost in the place.

"Same thing at the Desert Inn. They treated us like royalty. We stayed there when Scat was doing a *Charlie's Angels* segment with Dean Martin. We could walk right out of our room and into the casino.

"But back in those early days, it was really different. Somebody black finally opened a hotel on the black side of town, the Moulin Rouge. It was really plush. They had cards in the rooms giving you a chance to buy stock in the hotel for ten dollars a share. We stayed there until it went broke. What was funny was that you saw a lot of white people there; they came over to see all the mixed couples.

"Scat finally quit playing Las Vegas. He said he wasn't going to work in a place that wouldn't let blacks in. He didn't go back until things there had changed."

Playing in Las Vegas, however, did get Scatman invited to New York, where he performed at the Apollo in Harlem and at the Palace, among other places. In early March 1954, he was at the Apollo, still regarded at that time as the top of the mountain for black entertainers. He headlined a bill with Tiny Bradshaw's band that also featured several "New Acts" who never made it: Billy & Eleanor Byrd, Chuck Willis, George Williams, and Los Gatos. The movie feature was MGM's *Tall Target*. The reviewer for *Variety* wrote of Scatman's performance, which closed the show: "Crothers, who has netted a following through his stint on the Donald O'Connor tv'er and his recent appearance along Las Vegas bistro row, makes his first stand in New York. His vocal material is delivered with fine polish. His bop stylings are definitely his own, and when he does 'Ghost Riders' in the closing bit, he brings down the house. Other exceptional items are his clever parodies on the bigname vocalists and his turn at the drums."

At the end of March, he was at the Palace, billed beneath the Four Celleanos, Nivellis, Buddy Clayton, and Harris & Shore, but according to *Variety*, "Nearest item to a hit is Sherman ('Scat Man') Crothers, who has been wintering on the Donald O'Connor vidshows. Crothers, an experienced hand at singing, makes his mark with the crowd with a series of tunes engagingly worked over. He injects a mite of comedy with his version of 'Ghost Riders' and hits it off well with such odd tunes as 'Shiniest Mouth in Town' and his version of 'Walkin' My Baby Back Home.'"

The great advantage Scatman had was in having other talents, and other work, to fall back on when there didn't seem to be much call for his acting talents. That, and not being too proud to do whatever he needed to do to make a living.

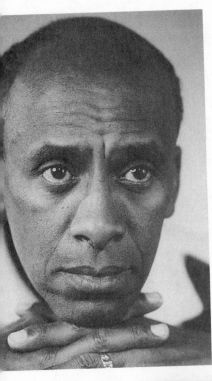

Scatman around 1938

Helen in 1941

Scatman's band in 1940—Vanetta Brown, singer; Jimmy Harris, sax (*fourth from left*), Milton Thomas, trumpet (*far right*); Duke Crowder, piano

At Billy Berg's—Duke Crowder, piano; Jimmy Harris, sax; Vic Macmillan, bass

Scatman on the stand-up cocktail drums. Oliver Michaux on piano.
Middle 1940s

Helen and Donna in the park, around 1950

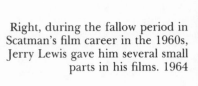

The part of Enoch in *Meet Me at the Fair* was Scatman's first major film role. The 1952 film also starred Dan Dailey and Chet Allen.

Right, during the fallow period in Scatman's film career in the 1960s, Jerry Lewis gave him several small parts in his films. 1964

In *The King of Marvin Gardens*, Scatman played Lewis, the head of a black mob in Atlantic City. His first film with Jack Nicholson, the 1972 release was also his favorite, for the role was a sustaining, dramatic one.

With Redd Foxx. Scatman's daughter, Donna, remembers that when she was growing up, the neighbors were not impressed with her father. A visit from Foxx, however, caused a neighborhood stir.

As Louie the Garbageman on *Chico and the Man,* Scatman finally got a seat on "the gravy train."

Below, Scatman played golf with Jack Albertson and helped shield the young star of *Chico,* Freddie Prinze, from the throngs of admirers who waited for him outside the NBC studios.

Left, in the TV drama special *The Sty of the Blind Pig*, Scatman and Maidie Norman played the roles of blacks living in Chicago in the late 1950s. After he started appearing in *Chico and the Man*, Scatman got many offers for other TV work.

Scatman with Jack Nicholson in *One Flew Over the Cuckoo's Nest*, a film in which much of Scatman's best work wound up on the cutting-room floor.

Scatman was the interlude pianist at a San Francisco cabaret in *The Cheap Detective* (1978), starring Peter Falk. His role in this film may have led to his being cast in the TV series *Casablanca*.

Scatman with John Wayne on the set of *The Shootist* (1976), Wayne's last film.

Showing all of his "104 teeth" and his trademark sunglasses, Scatman leans against his Cadillac, which sports one of his two "vanity" license plates.

Next to his role in *The King of Marvin Gardens*, the role of Doc Lynch in *Bronco Billy* was Scatman's favorite. He also enjoyed working with Clint Eastwood.

Scatman and his daughter, Donna, listen to Mayor Thomas Bradley read the proclamation of Scatman Crothers Day in Los Angeles, April 8, 1981.

Scatman, who did the voice of Meadowlark Lemon on the cartoon show *The Harlem Globetrotters,* appeared with Globetrotters Curley Neal and Geese and with Bob Denver in the 1981 TV special *The Harlem Globetrotters on Gilligan's Island.*

In *Twilight Zone—The Movie*, Scatman played Mr. Bloom, who teaches the residents of a nursing home how to recapture the freedom and wonder of childhood.

To the end of his life Scatman carried around his beat-up four-string Martin guitar and played it at every opportunity.

CHAPTER 6

OUT OF THE LIMELIGHT

DONNA CROTHERS DANIELS DIDN'T KNOW HER FATHER WELL in her early years. "I'm a little closer to my mother because I was around her more," she said in 1985. "He worked at night. We all sat and ate dinner together. He never put a bite of food in his mouth until he had said a prayer. He always made me eat my vegetables, and I hated that. But then he would start getting ready for work soon after that. I think he'd leave the house about eight o'clock. He worked a lot in Whittier at a club called Reuben's. So then I went to bed, and when I got up in the morning to go to school, he was asleep. He would have gotten in around two A.M., and my mother would get up and fix his breakfast at two or three in the morning. Of course, I was asleep. And then I got up, and Mother would fix my breakfast, and I'd be in school all day. When I came home from school, he'd be sleeping.

"I never resented that. I knew he had to work. That's the

way we ate, the way we survived. It wasn't like he was goofing off or anything. That was his schedule. That was our life.

"But on his days off, he'd take me places. I was told that he put me on a horse when I was two and a half. I love to horseback ride. He would take my girlfriends and me to Kiddieland. He took us to parks and zoos. I remember one time we found a little puppy, and we named it Pinky because it had a pink spot on its nose. My mother almost killed him. She said, 'Not another dog, noooo.' But he said, 'He was just wandering around on the street and he was lost and, honey, don't be mad, but . . .' So of course we got to keep him.

"I took piano lessons when I was a child. Also violin and ballet lessons, but I remember the piano lessons because he was trying to teach me to read music, and he had only just learned himself. Before that, he always just played by ear.

"I had fun with him, but my mother was really the one I always turned to. If my bike needed fixing, I'd take it to my mother. If a fuse blew, she'd replace it. She knew the trick of putting a penny behind the fuse. He'd say, 'Honey, the lights are out. Fuse? What's a fuse box? What is that? Oh, that's the thing near the washer and dryer.' He was not mechanically inclined. If the car didn't start, he'd say, 'Let's call somebody.' Most guys know about cars. They know the problem is the battery; they'll get jumper cables and go to work. But it was my mother would go out there and tinker and make it work. I think the best he ever did was change a light bulb. Bicycles, roller skates, anything . . . go to Mother.

"The house was always spotless, and she never minded when he would call up and say he was bringing some friends home for dinner. I remember on fight nights, my father would have three or four guys over, and they'd drink beer and watch the fight. They gave a lot of parties. I remember sneaking out and grabbing a little champagne and checking out all the people. They enjoyed their life."

Helen remembers those parties. "Ever since Donna was a little girl, I was giving parties. We lived in that house twenty-one years, and every holiday, every birthday, every occasion we could think of, we'd have a house full of people, and I'd cook turkeys, homemade dressing, hams, macaroni and cheese, brisket, fried chicken, big pies. I'd just cook and cook, and everybody used to go home with a 'people bag.' "

The guests at these parties were usually not famous. Most of the Crotherses' friends were just ordinary folk.

"He wasn't famous when I was growing up," says Donna. "He was working in supper clubs. He went out of town a lot. People had heard of him, but they'd say, 'Oh, he dances, or oh, he plays the piano.' But nobody really was impressed by him. I got more response when Redd Foxx came by the house.

"There was chaos when Redd Foxx came by. The neighbors would all be saying, 'That's Redd Foxx.' They never said, 'Hey, there's Scatman.' My father lived there constantly, so he was just a neighbor."

Helen recalls, "With Scat being out of town so much, there was just Donna and me. We had this big backyard and it was all fenced in, and all the neighborhood kids would come to play. At nine o'clock, everybody'd come to see if the gate's open, and every kid in the neighborhood would be in the yard, because I had swings and rides and slides and sandboxes. She had so many toys, her room looked like a May Company toy department. Every place Scat went, he'd send her a big lion, a big tiger, a doll, or something.

"I gave them all away, and now I regret it. She had one doll he sent her that had a black face and a white face. You'd look at it and it had a white face, and then you'd turn its head and it had a black face. You don't see those things very often. I don't know where he got it from. It would probably be worth some money today.

"Once in a while, Donna and I would go to wherever Scat was performing. I remember when she was four or five, we took a train to San Diego where he was working at the Top. She'd never been on a train before, and she was all dressed up. She went out into the aisle and danced, and everybody was applauding. We went down on the train and then we drove back with Scat."

"We had some good times. I'd take a carload of kids to Griffith Park. They used to have a little place called Tinker's Town, where they had little rides and ponies. Then later, I took her ice-skating, roller-skating, to children's plays.

"When she started school, I always used to pick her up and drop her off. One day, after we got home, she said, 'Mother, this little white girl, Linda, says her mother wants to know why I'm my color and you're white.' Instead of getting mad or making some nasty remark, I said, 'You go back and you tell Linda to tell her mother that we think every color is beautiful, that your mother is white and your father is a Negro—we said Negro then—and that's why you are your color.'

"We had a few incidents like that. Another time in the bank I had Donna with me. She was out in the sun a lot, so she was kind of brownish. This little white woman kept looking at Donna, looking at me, and then she'd smile—you know, one of those phony smiles. I finally said, 'Is there anything wrong?' She said, 'Are you taking care of her?' I said, 'Yes, I'm taking care of her, but not in the way you mean. She's mine, my flesh and blood. Her father is Negro, and I am white.' That was it."

Donna does not recall any instances of racism in her childhood. "In fact," she said in 1985, "I experienced the first racial confrontation of my life the other day at the gym. And I'm thirty-six years old. This white woman said, 'You don't talk to a white girl like that.' I said, 'I beg your pardon. Did you just get here? Are you from the South or what?' I said, 'Lady, I don't care if you're green or purple. If I have something to say, I'm going to say it.'

"When I was young, I never had any problems. Basically, that was because I look black. I am black. I went to black schools. All my friends were black.

"I was shy and introverted as a child, but that was because I was fat as a child. Now I'm at a nice weight, but back then I was really fat. I don't mean just heavy. In my day, they called fat girls TV Mamas, and that was my nickname. I was huge. My mother tried to put me on a diet, took me to the doctor. I got more negative reactions as a child because of my weight than I ever did because of their mixed marriage.

"I don't recall my father ever mentioning my weight, because he knew I was sensitive about it. My mother, on the other hand, was very concerned. She took me to doctors, gave me pills, packed me nutritional lunches. My father never said, 'Hey, you're getting big.' I don't know if that was beneficial or not. In my case, it probably would have been detrimental for my father to say, 'Oh, you're fat.' He loved me because I was me."

Donna recalls that when she was eight or nine years old, she traveled alone to Sacramento, where Scatman was appearing in *Finian's Rainbow,* his last foray into legitimate theater. It was the first time she had ever been on an airplane. "He was right there waiting for me when I got off the plane," she recalls, "looking worried and wondering where I was."

Another time, Helen took Donna and a girlfriend of hers to Hesperia, where Scatman was working at an inn. "We ordered room service like there was no tomorrow," Donna recalls. "We kept those waiters hopping. Trays were lined up outside in the hallway. We'd wake up in the middle of the night and order room service. We were two little girls who wanted everything we could get."

There were also trips to Las Vegas before Scatman stopped going there. "I couldn't see him because I couldn't go into the bar," she says. "My mother would have to pretend she was a patron. But I loved being around the pool.

"That wasn't a normal, everyday occurrence, of course. It was like a vacation. Once or twice a year, we'd join my father wherever he was playing."

Scatman played mostly at supper clubs in the Valley. His steadiest gig was at Reuben's in Whittier, where Helen remembers his group included Charles Cardwell on drums, but he played other clubs as well.

He recalled, "I was working at this ofay restaurant called the Concord House in the Valley, and I got a call to come to play the Parisian Room [at Washington and LaBrea in Los Angeles]. I

worked that place when they didn't want blacks in there, 1959
and '60. A lot of people don't know this, but I'm the cause of that
marquee being up there. Because when I was working with my
trio out in the Valley, Francis, the owner, used to come out and
romance me. He'd say, 'Scat, I'd like you to come into my club.
I've give you X amount of dollars.' I said, 'Francis, the money's
all right, but I can't come in there with those meat-market signs
on the wall—Scatman Crothers, two pounds for a dollar.' I said,
'Now, if you get me a marquee, I'll come in there.' So that's when
he got that marquee. Then, later, I said, 'Francis, you gotta get
some black bartenders and waiters in here. That's over, that old
prejudice. Now that area is about eighty percent black. He made
his money off of the blacks. It's one of the only places where you
can still hear true blues."

Although he hadn't done any steady television work since
The Colgate Comedy Hour, Scatman did a couple of guest spots in
television series in the late 1950s—on *Alfred Hitchcock Presents*
and on *Bourbon Street Beat.* He wasn't doing much recording, but
he did make an album for High Fidelity Records called *Rock 'n'
Roll with Scatman,* which included such songs as "Ghost Riders in
the Sky," "I Got Rhythm," "St. James Infirmary," and "September Song." "There was only one rock and roll tune on it, and that
was 'Nobody Knows Why,' " Scatman chuckled. He kept his hand
in a variety of entertainment venues.

He and Larry Finley remained close. "We'd do openings for
Thrifty Mart," Finley recalls. Clora Bryant, relatively unique in
the music business as a female trumpet player, was another musician whom Finley would call on at such times. She remembers,
"We used to play off the back of a truck at the opening of the
markets. They'd set the truck up, and we'd play. I remember I
did one over on Central Avenue for Adlai Stevenson when he
was running for president, but the one I did with Scat that sticks
in my mind was the opening of a market over at Crenshaw and
Jefferson, because it went over pretty big. Oh, and we also did
the opening of a Ford dealership on Crenshaw off Adams. Vivian Fears was playing piano with him then, and her husband,
Vernon Slater, was on sax. Scat would play his little guitar and

sing—he was singing 'The Shiniest Mouth in Town' at that time.

"It was a good way to pick up a couple of bucks. We were paid scale, but I don't remember if that was twelve dollars or twenty dollars. At that time, Larry had a radio show. Later on he did the same thing, but they televised it. Scat was on those, but I wasn't."

With Finley, Scatman also did charity appearances. Finley recalls, "We used to go out to the City of Hope. I started doing telethons around 1953 or 1954, and I always had Scat on them. Wherever I went, he was there, too. He always had his guitar, and that wonderful, wonderful smile. The audience would always scream for 'Ghost Riders in the Sky,' and the camera used to zoom right in on his mouth. That was live television. That wasn't the TV we see today where they rehearse and then put it on tape. We used to cold-conk it. I'd say, 'Scat, we got about six minutes to fill here,' and he'd do it. He was absolutely fantastic.

"I remember I did the *KNXT Fortieth Anniversary Special* from Kurtland's in Ontario, and every week Scat would go up there with me. We'd leave L.A. around nine at night, go on the air around eleven or midnight, and work right through until eight in the morning. He was never tired, always jovial, always happy.

"It got so every place I went, if Scatman wasn't with me, people would be disappointed. We traveled a lot together. So many times at the L.A. airport, the skycaps would look at me and say, 'I know you. What's your name?' I'd say, 'Larry Finley,' and they'd say, 'Oh, Scatman.'

"I remember one time we were in Yuma, Arizona, for a telethon we put on. He was so considerate of his family. When we arrived, the first thing he did was call Helen. He had to check in with Helen to make sure everything was all right and for her to know that he was all right. He did that everywhere we went."

"I left L.A. in 1960, but from the time we met up until the time I left, we were practically inseparable.

Finley knew Scatman was having a hard time making a living, and he did whatever he could to help out his friend. "I got him a week's engagement at the Little Club, which is very elite. They used to have Joan Rivers there when she first started. I had to really convince Marsha Ledson to put Scatman in for a week, because it was a white club, but she finally gave in, and Scat was a smash. I think Scat had a great deal to do with the breaking down of racism out there [in Los Angeles]. He was really beautiful inside, and he was so giving, and as long as he made people happy, that's all he cared about. I always thought he was put on this earth to make people happy; he had that nature."

Although Scatman was not earning much money, he helped friends out as much as he could. Helen recalls, "There was a guy named Al Williams, who's dead now. He was one of the Step Brothers back in the 1930s and forties, but he hadn't worked much in some years. We used to give him food, and when he'd show up at the door asking to borrow money for gas, I'd give it to him. Scat gave him a job. He called him his manager, but he was actually a kind of gofer. He would carry Scat's guitar case and set up his music stand and things like that. Scat didn't need him to do that, but he knew Al needed the job."

When approached for a loan, Scatman would usually try his best. Sometimes he would get the money back, sometimes he would not. Says Helen, "I'd say to him, 'We've lost a lot of money over the years. But he'd say to me, 'Honey, the Devil will get his due.' "

Scatman was not one to press for repayment of loans he had made. But Helen recalls one exception. "There was this guy, a piano player, well known now. He came by and wanted a loan of fifty dollars. He had a little office over on Wilshire Boulevard, and he was behind on his rent or something like that. Scat always said, 'Well, you'll have to talk to my wife. She handles the money.' Well, the guy keeps talking. They're going to turn his lights off, they're going to disconnect his phone. Pretty soon the fifty-dollar loan has turned into a two-hundred-fifty-dollar loan. But I gave him the money. He said he'd pay it back in three months.

"Three months went by, and he didn't pay it back. He started getting successful, playing Vegas. Every time I asked about the money, he put me off. One day, I called him, and he said, 'You'll get it when I get it.' He called me a name, and then Scat got mad. I had Scat go out and find his car—he was driving a Jaguar—and get the license-plate number, and I attached his car. I had to go to court to get that money back.

"But Scat was so generous. One time he was at the market doing some shopping for me and he saw this homeless man. The guy asked him for a dollar. Scat looked down at the man's shoes and saw that his feet were coming out of them. He said, 'What size shoe do you wear?' and it was Scat's size. Scat told him, 'You wait right here,' and he went home and got four pairs of his shoes and gave them to the man. Then he gave him ten dollars and said, 'Now don't go spending this on food. You can get food at one of the churches. You take this money and get yourself a room.' The man, who was white, looked at Scat's license plate, which said 'Blest,' and he said, 'You *are* blessed.' "

In 1957, Scatman and his trio hooked up with the USO and went on frequent overseas trips to entertain at military installations in Korea, Hawaii, Guam, Manila, and Hong Kong. The tours were organized by Johnny Grant and included Connie Stevens and Valerie Harper among the attractions. The pay was good, the work was fairly steady, and Scatman enjoyed the opportunity to entertain the troops with versions of his time-tested variety show, in which he sang, played drums and guitar and ukulele, made up silly songs, and played bop and pop tunes with his sidemen. Part of the entertainment was his outfits—one of his favorites was a zoot-suit style "vanilla rouge" number—cream-colored with red flecks as well as piping around lapels and pockets. He performed with the USO well into the middle 1960s, and it may have been in this context that he and Bob Hope first met. Neither man could remember whether it was the USO or golf that first brought them together.

Scatman had resisted golf for decades. "I thought it was a silly game," he recalled in 1985. "Leonard Firestone tried to get me into it way back in 1939–40 when I was playing at Harry's Black and Tan in Akron, Ohio. The Nicholas Brothers tried to get me to play in '45 and '46. Even Floyd Ray. He had a hell of a band years ago in the late thirties and forties. He used to try to get me to play. I said, 'Man, I don't want to play that silly game.'

Billy Eckstine used to try to get me to play in the forties. But I didn't want any part of it."

According to Teddy Edwards, whose friendship with Scatman had begun in the middle 1940s, it was he who first got Scat on a golf course.

"It was the first time I really worked with him on a job. It was 1958 or 1959, and we were at this cowboy place down in Colton, California. I was with him and George Bledsoe on bass and Yvonne Williams on piano—we were a group. We would drive down there every night and drive back every night. I was playing golf during that time; in fact, I was almost supporting my family by playing golf, I was a kind of golf hustler. So by the time I'd get in the car every night on the way to work, I'd fall asleep."

"Scat said, 'Is it really that much fun? You stay out there all day, tired when you get home?' So I talked him into going to the driving range with me out here on Rodeo Road and La Cienega, and it became really important to his life. He really appreciated it through the years. He got a chance to play with the celebrities in all the tournaments. He used to give me boxes of golf balls— the Wilson sporting-goods company used to give him equipment. He called me 'Teach' on the golf course."

Recalled Scatman, "I decided to give it a try, and I never looked back. It's a game that's up to you and you alone. It's your challenge and nobody else's. That's why I like the game. Every club in that golf bag is for a certain shot due to the elements."

It took some time for him to develop his game. He liked to joke, "I'd been playing about two years, and one day I played a new course. Some guy asked me after, 'Scat, how'd you like the course?' I told him, 'I don't know, I wasn't on it.' But I learned about golf—you drive for show and you putt for dough."

Scatman eventually managed to stay on a golf course. "I play a good game," he'd say, although he quoted different handicaps. One time, he described his handicap as "an honest fifteen." Another time, he said, "I have a fourteen handicap, which means I shoot in the low eighties. If it gets any hotter than that, I don't play."

By the 1960s, he was in demand at celebrity golf tournaments. "Every year we went to Vegas to play in the golf tournaments," Helen recalls. "We'd go to Palm Springs two or three times a year. We'd go to San Diego for the Andy Williams Open. He played all the tournaments—Dinah Shore's, Sammy Davis, Jr.'s, the Bob Hope Desert Classic. I traveled with him most of the time, because it was different from when he was working."

Golf, his family, and making a living were what occupied Scatman in the 1960s. While he kept up with the progress of the civil-rights movement, he did not become actively involved. His ideas on equal rights had been set a long time back, and he saw no reason to alter his stance, or change his activities. He was aware that older blacks like him were now frequently called Uncle Toms, but he tried to take such remarks in stride, realizing that there was an ebb and flow to black political attitudes. He was more likely to joke about the prevailing militant black political winds than to get defensive about them. Showing up with an Afro wig was more his style than arguing with young Turks about black nationalism. One of his favorite lines was, "I was colored long before you were black."

Both Scatman and Helen were far more concerned about the rebellion of their daughter than about the talk of revolution among young black militants. For the most part, Donna had always been a well-behaved child. She recalls being spanked only two or three times in her life, and her major rebellion in her young years was refusing to eat her vegetables.

"I remember one time I just sat there and would not eat," she says. "And he was going to sit there until I did. I knew he was going to have to get up and go to work. What was he going to do, not go to work to make me eat my vegetables? I knew he had to go to work, and eventually he did.

"But when I was fourteen, fifteen, sixteen, I just totally rebelled. No, I'm not going to eat my vegetables. No, I'm not going to sit and have dinner if I'm not hungry. Of course, my mother took the brunt of it because she was there more. She'd say, 'Wait until your father gets home.' But by the time he got home, I was asleep, and he was not going to wake me up at two

o'clock in the morning to chastise me for something I did earlier."

"I wanted to get out, and I got married very young. Let's
just say I was too young to know better. My parents didn't care
for that at all. It's not that they didn't care for the person, because they never really got a chance to know him before I got
married. I just said, 'I'm going to get married,' and I did. So they
decided if I was really that determined and if I really thought
that was going to make me happy, they would accept it."

Helen even bought the young couple a house nearby—"a
beautiful little house with a fenced-in backyard and a nursery,"
she says. Soon Donna was living in the house by herself, since the
marriage did not work out. "I did it, and I regretted it," says
Donna, who remained in the house alone for some time because
she did not want to admit defeat and go back home.

Not long after Donna's marriage broke up, blacks in the
Watts section of Los Angeles rioted in 1964. Helen recalls, "Scat
was with the USO in Korea entertaining the troops when the
riots started. It was just two blocks west of where we lived, on
Rodeo Road and Exposition Street. He was over there entertaining the troops, and they started burning buildings two blocks
away. They burned one of Scat's favorite rib joints, they burned
the bank and broke out all the windows. They burned down the
dress store right on the corner, and there I was a white woman
in an all-black neighborhood. I thought, If they come over here,
they'll kill me.

"At night there was a curfew; at seven P.M. the big army
truck would come down to the end of our block and park, and
the soldiers would stand there with their big guns, and they
wouldn't let any cars up the street, and you couldn't get out.
They didn't let anybody but the doctor and the fire department
in. You had to be somebody important to be let past.

"We had such wonderful friends. There was a black lady
who died just recently. She called me and said, 'Helen, don't
leave the house.' She said they were saying, 'Whitey, Whitey, kill
Whitey.' She said, 'If you need anything, my husband or I will go
to the store for you.'

"There was a woman out in Woodland Hills who knew Scat from when he used to work at a little club out there. She called him, and I said he was out of town. She said, 'Mrs. Crothers, we would like you to come over and stay with us until this riot is over. We'll come and pick you up.' But I had three dogs and a cat, and I didn't know who would take care of them, so I stayed where I was.

"A little black kid named Skipper lived down the street, and he went to the store for me. I had my gun—Scat always made sure I had a gun for protection when he was away. But I was worried about Donna. She was by herself. I gave her one of my guns to keep for a while, and then finally I said, 'Go get all your stuff, bring your dogs.' You should have seen our house. The big dog was in her bedroom. Her cats were in there. I was afraid her cats were going to fight with my cats. I would run to the store and come back with these big bags of dog food, cat food. When we wanted to go out, I would take all my dogs and put them in the garage and lock her dogs in the bedroom.

"There was a radio call-in show on at the time, *The Ray Breen Show*. A lot of white people were calling up to say that the black people who were causing all this trouble ought to go back to Africa. So I got on the phone. I waited three hours before I got on. I said, 'Let me tell you something about black people.' I said, 'There are good and bad in every race. I'm Caucasian, and I know a lot of good black people. As a matter of fact, my husband is black, and we've been married twenty-eight years, and right now he's not in Watts rioting, he's overseas entertaining our United States troops.' Then a lot of people started calling me, because they recognized my voice. I said, 'Well, I don't care, just so those bigots don't recognize my voice.' I was so mad. There Scat was entertaining the troops, and these white people had the nerve to talk about blacks going back to Africa."

But life at Thirty-eighth and Cimmaron was never the same for Helen after that. She felt considerable hostility in the black neighborhood where she had lived without fear for many years. She recalls, "One day I got out of my car over on LaBrea and Rodeo Road. I was going to the drugstore, and I passed this little black boy, who was about eight or nine. He said, 'Hey, hey Whit-ey.' At first I just kept going, then I turned around. I said, 'Wait a minute, I want to talk to you. I said, 'How would you like it if someone walked up to you and said, "Hey, hey Blackie?"'

"He said, 'I wouldn't like it.' I pulled out my wallet and showed him a picture of Donna. I said, 'Look, this is my daughter, and she's the same color as you.' He said, 'Why?' I said, 'Because my husband is a black man. His name is Scatman Crothers.' This little boy knew who Scat was and got all excited, wanted to know when Scat was going to be in a movie or on television. He ended up walking me to the Thrifty's.

"Around the same time, a new family moved in next to us on Thirty-eighth Street. They were ignorant people. One day, as I was walking out to my car, they started singing, 'Whitey, Whitey, long live Whitey.' I just ignored it. But Scat didn't like that at all. He started talking about moving, but things quieted down and we stayed."

Donna moved back in with her parents not long after her brief marriage fell apart. She had little desire to follow in her father's footsteps and be an entertainer. She'd shown some aptitude in music over the years, and had taken both piano and violin for a while. She also had a very good voice. But she was not interested in a career in music.

When Donna was about fifteen, Scatman was approached about her being a regular on a television series. "They wanted a young black girl," says Helen Crothers, "and they offered five hundred a week, which was pretty good pay for a fifteen-year-old. But she said she didn't want to do it, and Scat said, 'Honey, if you don't want to do it, don't do it.' "

The early 1960s had been no better for Scatman's film work than the late fifties had been. In 1960, he had appeared in *The Sins of Rachel Cade* for Warner Bros. Starring Angie Dickinson, Peter Finch, and Roger Moore, it was set in the African Congo (now Zaire) and involved the efforts of a nurse to win the trust of the locals. Several black actors had small roles as Africans, among them Woody Strode, Juano Hernandez, Frederick O'Neal, and Rafer Johnson, the Olympic decathlon winner. Scatman played Musinga, which gives some idea of what he did in the film.

It was four years before he got another part in a movie, a bit part in a shock melodrama for Paramount starring Olivia de Havilland titled *Lady in a Cage*. That same year, billed as the Shoeshine Boy, he polished Jerry Lewis's big toenail in *The Patsy* for Paramount.

"I worked on the picture for about five weeks, and during that five weeks I really picked up on this cat," said Scatman. "I had never met him. I wrote a tune about him called "Jerry," and part of it went like this:

"If you are in Hollywood
And would like to make a movie
There's a guy that you should know
Who's so kind, and very groovy
That is why I sing this song
Self experience can't be wrong
Once you work with him for a day
Then you too will say
It's Jerry, Jerry
I mean Lewis, shoobedobopbop"

The friendship that developed between the two benefited both. Scatman began appearing on Lewis's telethons for muscular dystrophy, and in return Lewis made sure that Scatman got small parts in several of his films. In 1965, he had a small role in another Jerry Lewis film for Paramout, *The Family Jewels,* and in 1966 he appeared briefly in Lewis's first film for Columbia, *Three on a Couch*. But for Lewis, Scatman would have had no film work at all in the middle 1960s.

For a brief time, he did host a talent show on local television. "It was like that show Ed McMahon has now," says Helen. "I think it was called *Just For Kicks*. New acts would be auditioned, and every week different acts would be showcased, and the audience picked the winner."

Helen remembers that a woman acquaintance called her

during the run of the show to report that Scatman's eyes were "bugging out" at all the beautiful young girls who auditioned to be on the show. Says Helen, "I told her, 'That's what his eyes are for. Why shouldn't he appreciate beautiful young girls? Don't call me to tell me he's looking at them. If you see him checking into a motel with one of them, then you call me.' "

The show was short-lived, and Scatman waited through another fallow period until the new decade began. He recorded a comedy album titled "Comedy Sweepstakes." He also appeared briefly in 20th Century–Fox's *Hello, Dolly,* directed by Gene Kelly and starring Barbra Streisand and Louis Armstrong. The title song would become a megahit for Armstrong.

Otherwise, Scatman's only film work was the voice of Scat Cat in the Walt Disney animated film *The Aristocats.* The film, about an eccentric, wealthy Frenchwoman who leaves her fortune to her cat, Duchess, and her three kittens, featured a large, star-studded cast. Maurice Chevalier was the narrator, Eva Gabor was Duchess, Sterling Holloway did the voice of Roquefort, Scatman was Scat Cat, a hip alley-cat bandleader who swings on the Left Bank of Paris, and Scatman's old friend and fellow Hoosier Phil Harris was O'Malley, also the leader of a jazz band, which jammed with that of Scat Cat.

"We never were in the studio at the same time," says Harris. "The way they did it was one person at a time read his script. I never even saw Eva Gabor, and she was the star. Nowadays, they tell me, they have the whole cast—they do it together, and everybody's got a mike. But when Disney did it, we were all recorded separately. In *Jungle Book,* I never saw Louis Prima, and yet in the film we did two numbers together, line for line, back and forth."

Called by one reviewer the last of the high-quality Disney cartoon features, the film was one that Walt Disney himself had helped conceive in 1963, and it had taken a total of four years to make.

Recalled Scatman, "I worked for three years on *The Aristocats* with Disney. That was his last film. A lot of work goes into animated films. Most people would be surprised. I was the voice for Scat Cat. Remember him? I love doing cartoons because I love children."

In the meantime, Scatman was still appearing in local clubs and traveling to out-of-town engagements with some frequency. Fletcher Smith joined him around 1965. Three years younger than Scatman, he had been playing professionally since 1928. "I've been playing sixty-one years, and I have worked with everybody," he said in 1990. "I remember when Scatman came out here in the forties; Billy Berg sent for him. I gigged with him around town for years.

"In the 1960s, Scat had a trio, and I joined him then. A guy named Chuck Hamilton was the bass player. Scat was on the drums. We played and sang—Scat didn't do any comedy routines then. We played a lot of places—Reuben's, the Sherman Room in Buena Park, up in Stockton at a Chinese place. We worked in Lake Tahoe and in Dallas, Texas, at the Playboy Club."

"He was good to work for. He paid us more than scale—I always worked for more than scale. He paid for the uniforms— we wore business suits. For transportation, sometimes we'd drive and sometimes we'd fly. Everybody in the group had a car. It was just according to how far it was. When we had to stay overnight out of town, we made our own arrangements; we didn't worry about things like that. He was a good musician. We were all good musicians. I handled most all the music and did all the arranging."

"On any job, we had a routine—certain numbers we'd play. If the audience requested a number, we'd interrupt our routine and play it for them. We never practiced—we were all musicians, didn't need to practice. We had a ball working together."

While not famous, Scatman the musician had a loyal following. He was a consummate performer, and his warm personality gained him new followers wherever he went. Around 1967, he was the first black performer to be booked into the Forge in Glendale, an all-white enclave that may well have never hosted any other black performer before. "They thought I was crazy," he chuckled. But he did great business. His act was reviewed in the local newspaper—probably the first time that newspaper had ever run a review of a black act. Scatman later performed at the Melody Room in Glendale.

Scatman had a way of enveloping his audiences with warmth. Actress Carol Speed remembers seeing him for the first time at the Roxy in late 1971.

"I was doing a segment of *Sanford and Son* called 'Here Comes the Bride, There Goes the Bride,' " she says. "I was supposed to marry Demond [Wilson], but I leave him standing at the altar. It was a really great segment, and all the actors really meshed together. So after the taping, Redd [Foxx] suggested that we all go to see Scatman at the Roxy on Sunset Boulevard. He and Scatman were extremely good friends.

"This was very exciting to me—hanging out with Redd and the other actors from *Sanford and Son*, my first time at the Roxy, and my first time seeing Scatman.

"We were seated at the best table in the club, because Redd was such a big star on television at that time. Scatman came over to the table to greet Redd. Talk about warm and beautiful! He was a man of great talent but very humble. It's like he knew his talent was a blessing from God, and when he went onstage to perform, it's like all of his beauty just flowed through everyone there. Very few entertainers can reach that magnitude of purity in their music. It was like he had a secret about life that we could only guess at! From that moment on, I've always put the gift of any talent I have above all other things that I might encounter in life."

Perhaps because of his work on *The Aristocats*, which was released in 1970, Scatman got more work in TV cartoons, providing the voice for Meadowlark Lemon on the Hanna-Barbera cartoon series *The Harlem Globetrotters*, which originally ran from September 12, 1970, to September 2, 1972, and which aired again in 1978.

Scatman was a natural for cartoon-voice work, for it was the expressions of the actors who did the voices that inspired the animators to create the cartoon characters to go along with the voices. Few actors in Hollywood had faces as expressive as Scatman's.

Or Phil Harris's. He recalls, "I used to say to the animators, 'With all the many voices you have to draw from, how come you picked me?' They said, 'Well, Phil, there's a lot of people with tremendous voices and a lot of talent, but they have no expression. We can't get anything from them.' See, the animators sat in the booth and watched your expression when you delivered the lines, and then they started drawing their characters. We used to do like four sides of dialogue and it would take them three months to catch up with it."

Scatman appeared in two more films with 1970 release dates. One was *The Great White Hope,* with a screenplay by Howard Sackler based on his award-winning Broadway play about the black prizefighter Jack Johnson. James Earl Jones, who had starred on Broadway, also starred in the film, whose cast included Jane Alexander as Johnson's white mistress, Etta, and an interesting group of black veteran actors and actresses, among them Beah Richards, Moses Gunn, and William Walker. Scatman played a carnival barker in one of the scenes in which Johnson was reduced to sideshow work.

The other 1970 film was *Bloody Mama,* a sleazy story about Ma Barker, leader of the legendary Barker gang, starring Shelley Winters and released by American International Pictures. Scatman played a character named Moses.

After yet more bit parts in *Chandler* (1971), an MGM picture starring Warren Oates and Leslie Caron (Scatman played the character named Smoke), *Open Shadow,* and *Another Day at the Races,* Scatman decided to get an agent whose work was concentrated in the film industry. He contacted Don Schwartz.

"I'm not sure exactly how we started working together," said Schwartz in 1986. "I think Scat just called me out of the blue and said he wanted somebody to represent him. I remember I didn't know who he was. Maybe the music media or nightclub media might have known him well, and a few of the in-crowd, but I don't think he was that well known. I remember him coming in to the office and sitting on a chair on the side wall, and he had to wait for a long time, but he was very patient. He held some things on his lap, probably pictures, and he sat there, and I had to let him wait because of something. When I did get to talk with him, I said, 'You're an interesting character type.' In fact, the only reason why I decided to take him on was because he was a good character type.

"I went to see him perform at some club, and I couldn't believe it. He did things like 'The Sheik of Araby' and 'The Biscuit Song,' and I said to myself, 'This has got to be the most consummate entertainer of them all.' His timing was perfection. His choice of music was nostalgic and funny. I knew then that this was somebody that had more than just character.

"The first job he got through us was a one-day job in something with Jennifer Jones. He played a pianist. Then we got him some television exposure."

In 1971, Scatman appeared in guest spots on several television series, including "Eddie Joe" on the series *Nichols,* "Butterfield Ate 3526" on *The Good Life,* and "Three Men and a Witch on a Horse" on *Bewitched.* The following year, he was on *Disney on Parade,* a special.

Also in 1971, Scatman got a role in the first venture into films of the Motown Corporation, *Lady Sings the Blues,* the story of singer Billie Holiday. Obviously a vehicle put together by Motown president Berry Gordy for his favorite recording artist, Diana Ross, the film was much better than predicted. Ross performed admirably, and there was great chemistry between her and Billy Dee Williams, who played a composite of Holiday's many boyfriends. The movie also represented a breakthrough of sorts in film history by presenting a realistic romantic relationship between a black man and woman, who meet, court, fight, make up. The film was nominated for four Academy Awards. Ross was nominated for an Oscar as Best Actress, proving that she could be taken seriously as an actress.

Scatman's part as Big Ben, a "john," was small, but in Don Schwartz's opinion it proved to be a turning point in his film career. "She [Holiday] was going to become a lady of the night, and he was going to be her first customer," Shwartz recalls. "He comes in and starts to undress and he's telling her how he is going to ride the saddle like his pappy taught him. He created most of the dialogue, incidentally. He made it rhyme and so forth. And then while he was undressing, she was dressing, and then all of a sudden she says good-bye.

"I thought it was a good scene, but I didn't realize it was going to get so many people talking about him. I watched the film a couple more times. Then I got hold of a tape of it and kept watching, and then I said, 'No wonder.' He was so good in that— his timing, his fun, his black humor. It kind of snuck up on us—his success because of that film. I didn't even realize what was happening. But the calls started coming in."

While he was pleased to have got some recognition for his work in *Lady Sings the Blues,* on reflection, Scatman was not so pleased about his role in the film or about what he had done to make his "john" character so convincing. Helen recalls, "He used the word 'titties,' and he was sorry he did. He started thinking about all the children who knew his voice from cartoons, and he was afraid they might recognize his voice in the movie. After that, he decided not to take any more roles like that."

Although he could ill afford to do so, Scatman turned down several jobs. Helen recalls that he was offered a part in a film that had "a lot of bad, nasty words in it. He said, 'No, I'm not gonna do that. What kind of image would it make of me for the children who watch all those cartoons I've made?' "

Don Schwartz remembered, "He was offered a role opposite Dustin Hoffman. The part was sort of an effeminate guy, and he didn't take it. I think there was another role in a film in which there was a lot of nudity, and he wouldn't take that either."

According to Donna, Scatman would not even accept a chicken commercial, since he would not eat chicken. "My mother told me that years ago someone gave him some undercooked chicken, and ever since then he refused to eat it. Someone offered him a chicken commercial, and he said, 'Can't I eat something else?' They said, 'No, you have to eat the product on TV.' He said, 'No, I can't do it. I won't do it. It's not worth the money.' "

Scatman had his principles and never deviated from them, something rare in Hollywood.

He did not, however, want to be confined to happy-go-lucky roles, and when he was offered a part as a gangster in *The King of Marvin Gardens*, a 1972 Columbia release, he decided to take it.

The film is set in the decaying playground of Atlantic City in the gray, wintry off-season. Jack Nicholson played the artist brother who delivers monologues on late-night radio. Bruce Dern was the charismatic promoter brother who fronts black gangsters. Scatman was Lewis, the big boss of those gangsters. Identified in the credits as Benjamin "Scatman" Crothers, he was clearly not regarded by the show's producers as someone whose nickname would be immediately recognizable, although the reviewer for the *Hollywood Reporter* wrote that "he still has a strong screen presence." Scatman didn't care how he was billed; he was just happy to be featured throughout a film for a change. Understandably, it became his favorite role and continued to be.

Playing a local character who has mastered the Numbers game, Scatman could bring some experience to the role. He was also allowed some offhand witty moments that leavened the overall bleakness of the film. It could have been very important for his career, but unfortunately the film was not well received by critics. Pauline Kael called it an "indecipherable, dark-toned movie about brothers and spurious goals and the American Dream." Scatman disagreed with that characterization. "Bob Rafaelson [the director] was ahead of his time," said Scatman. "It was a big movie in England."

By the late 1960s, young whites were listening to black music, finding it chic to understand black street talk, and eager to hear anti-establishment dicta from blacks. Black kids, meanwhile, had been identified as significant film consumers. In 1969 alone, Hollywood supplied this new market with four different black movies—*Uptight*, *Slaves*, *The Learning Tree*, and *Putney Swope*.

The films that were critically well received did poorly at the box office, proving to filmmakers that audiences didn't especially want edification. Thus was ushered in the era of black action movies, beginning with Ossie Davis's 1970 *Cotton Comes to Harlem*, a cops-and-robbers farce, and epitomized by *Shaft*, directed by Gordon Parks and starring Richard Roundtree.

In 1972 there was an explosion of such films, disapprovingly called "blaxploitation movies" by Roy Wilkins of the NAACP, including *Shaft's Big Score, Top of the Heap, The Legend of Nigger Charley, Slaughter, Blacula, Blackenstein,* and *Superfly.*

Critics, especially liberal whites and middle-class blacks, charged that these films exploited blacks—hence the nickname—by glorifying the least desirable elements in the black community. But black actors and actresses were delighted to get the work, and studied up on gangster and superfly roles.

In his work in *The King of Marvin Gardens,* Scatman proved he could play a gangster type convincingly, but unfortunately he was passed over by the makers of most of the 1970s black gangster movies. The greatest result of his work in the film was his burgeoning friendship with Jack Nicholson, with whom he shared a liking for marijuana.

In 1979, in an interview for *Valley* magazine, Stephen Swain mentioned that Jack Nicholson talked openly about using marijuana and asked if Scatman agreed with Nicholson. Scatman replied, "Sure, it's good for you. That's one of my secrets. I've really been smoking 'shit' for at least 50 years. You see what the Bible says, 'He causes the grass to grow for the cattle and the herb for the services of man.' It's nothing but an herb. You don't have to do any processing, the Lord just plants it. And it's good for glaucoma, anything that ails you. It's good for everything. It makes you think beautiful thoughts. It's just good for you."

In 1985, after looking over the proposal for what was then to be his autobiography, Scatman had second thoughts about being so open about his use of marijuana and asked that the reference to it be deleted from the proposal for the book. When reminded that he had been quoted in *Valley,* he agreed to leave it in, but asked that a further religious reference he had made be deleted because he felt it was sacrilegious.

Whatever the reasons for their friendship, Nicholson promised him a role in his next movie. Naturally, Scatman was grateful, because film work paid well, and he could always use the money, not to mention the exposure. By the time Nicholson made good on his offer, however, Scatman was getting the best exposure of his career.

In 1972, Scatman appeared on the *Adam 12* TV series as well as *Love American Style*. The following year he was so busy with TV work that he had to disband the trio and stop playing clubs. He did guest shots on a number of TV series: *Temperatures Rising, Kojack, Ironside,* and *Faraday and Company*. He performed in the TV special *Moments with Dora,* as Reuben Hammer in the short-lived TV series *Griff,* starring Lorne Greene, and a pilot for former football star Roosevelt Grier called *Big Daddy*.

He still was not getting much film work. Steve Tisherman, who worked at the Don Schwartz Agency as a specialist in voice-overs before forming his own commercial agency, remembers that Scatman turned down some roles in "blaxploitation" films because he did not want to mar his wholesome image. But as time went on, he did accept some roles that he might not have considered earlier.

One was that of the character Cleveland in *Slaughter's Big Rip-Off,* a 1973 American International release starring Jim Brown, which openly copied the successful *Shaft* of 1971. In it, Brown plays Slaughter, an ex–Green Beret whose parents are murdered in Cleveland by the mob and who sets out to avenge their deaths.

In release that same year was *Detroit 9000,* in which Scatman played Reverend Markham, a small role in another cops-and-robbers film that featured a black cop (Hari Rhodes) and a white cop (Alex Rocco) battling the forces of urban corruption. Scatman later said, "That was a terrible movie, the bottom. I wasn't doing anything, so I took the part. It was filmed on Belle Isle, and I stayed at the Sheraton. While I was there, I did a telethon for retarded children with Soupy Sales as emcee. I played golf in a ladies' tournament there."

At least the role of Pop Byrd in *Black Belt Jones* was a substantial one. The Warner Bros. 1974 release starred black-belt karate champion Jim Kelly. Pop Byrd owns a karate school in a section of Watts scheduled for redevelopment. The mob wants to control the area and leans on Pop, accidentally killing him. His daughter Sidney, played by Gloria Hendry, happens to be a kung fu expert and helps Black Belt Jones (Kelly) bring the mobsters to justice.

Truck Turner was another such film. A 1974 American International Pictures release, it starred Isaac Hayes, Yaphet Kotto, Annazette Chase, Nichelle Nichols, Paul Harris, Stan Shaw, and a host of other black actors and actresses, most of them one-third Scatman's age. In it, bounty hunter Truck Turner (Hayes) is after Gator (Harris), a vicious pimp hood. Scatman played Duke, Turner's friend, who alerts Truck that Gator is also being sought by a big-shot gangster played by Yaphet Kotto.

Departing from the black action-film genre that year, he also made a brief appearance in a little-known release titled *Linda Lovelace for President,* in which the star of *Deep Throat* played the candidate of the Upright People's Party.

Scatman's TV work made up for the unsatisfying progress he was making in films. He appeared on *Sanford and Son, The Night Stalker, Toma, Mannix, McMillan and Wife,* and *The Odd Couple.* He did a TV special, *The Sty of the Blind Pig.*

He also did one of his most successful voices for a cartoon show, creating the voice of Hong Kong Phooey on the Hanna-Barbera cartoon series of the same name. The story followed the exploits of the crime-fighting dog Penrod Pooch, whose secret identity was that of Hong Kong Phooey: "Yah-hay-hoo and a rinky-dink to you! I'm Hong Kong Phooey, quicker than the human eye." The show aired on ABC from September 7, 1974, to September 4, 1976, although the second season on ABC was entirely reruns. No matter. The show was a great success. NBC then picked it up and ran it in 1978, 1979, and 1981, and it can still be seen on local stations around the country. Helen Crothers continues to collect residuals. Perhaps more than any other work he did, Scatman's work as Hong Kong Phooey endeared him to children.

CHAPTER 7

SCATMAN'S BIG BREAK

ONE DAY IN EARLY 1974, James Komack, producer of *Chico and the Man,* a new half-hour sitcom on NBC, called the Crothers house. Later to be the producer of *Welcome Back, Kotter,* Komack, who was an ex–jazz drummer, had known Scatman slightly for about three years and liked him immensely.

"I answered the phone," says Helen, "and he explained who he was. He said, 'We'd like Scat to come out and read for a part, and I know it's going to be him.' I turned it over to Don Schwartz, Scat's agent."

"I'd never heard of it [the show]," said Scatman in 1978, " 'cause I'd been working at night with my trio. So I said, 'Okay, I'll come out and read.' They liked what I read."

James Komack remembered the audition well: "I think his first line was something like, 'Hey, I'm here to pick up your garbage.' You know, Scat doesn't talk too clearly, and it came out something like 'Hey, Ahmhereafuhyhgatch.' I said, 'What'd he say?' Then I said, 'Hire him!' It was his *energy*, his vitality, that's incredible, tremendous, and he projects it. With one line, that man can *score*. His scenes are always upbeat. He *pushes* them up—by sheer force of all that energy."

Chico and the Man, which had premiered the previous fall, starred a young comedian named Freddie Prinze and veteran character actor Jack Albertson. The show was an immediate success. Prinze was an attractive young man who as the fast-talking, optimistic Chico Rodriguez managed to endear himself to the TV audience in much the same way he had done at the Comedy Club and other venues where he first attracted attention as a stand-up comedian emulating the late comedian Lenny Bruce. (At one time, Prinze was even engaged briefly to Bruce's daughter, Kitty.) He was also a great fan of Richard Pryor. Only eighteen and a high school dropout, he was the proverbial overnight success.

The show itself was a breakthrough of sorts in that it was the first series set in a Mexican-American neighborhood, the barrio of East Los Angeles. Trouble was, Prinze was not a Chicano, but Hungarian and Puerto Rican; or "Hungarican," as he liked to put it. The show was thus criticized by many Chicano organizations because there were no Chicanos in the cast.

Responding to this criticism, Komack brought on two Mexican-Americans: Isaac Ruiz as Ramón (Mando), Chico's friend, and Rodolfo Hoyos as Rudy, Ed's pal. He also decided to add a couple of black characters, Louie the Garbageman, and Mabel, a letter carrier. Mabel was played by Bonnie Boland. Scatman got the role of Louie.

Initially, the part of Louie was just an occasional role, for which Scatman received $750 a week. But from the moment he wandered into Ed's garage, Louie the Garbageman, with his twinkling eyes and ear-to-ear smile, proved to be very popular with the audience.

Scatman wrote Louie's signature song himself:

I'm the man who empties your can
So stick out your can. . . .

'cause here comes the garbage man!
I read a garbage can
like a Gypsy reads tea leaves
'Cause you are what you throw out.
Jabba-dee-boom!

Actually, he did not write that song for the show; "I've been singing 'Stick Out Your Can' with a real bluesy edge for years," he said.

By the time the season ended, all the other characters who had been added on were gone. Scatman was promoted to a regular.

"When they first hired him, they didn't know they were going to use him as a regular," says Don Schwartz. "They paid him seven-hundred-fifty dollars a week, because that was the top of the show for guest stars. Then they started wanting him as a regular, and they said they wanted to sign him to a contract, but still at seven-hundred-fifty dollars a week."

"Now, I thought he should get more than that as a regular, and so did he. But they held out. They told him he was missing shows, that I was dragging my feet. But Scatman trusted me. I think that's when he learned to trust me. He stood by me and said go ahead. He showed his solidarity with me. He'd say, 'We'll put our heads together like we're talking about something serious. Let's worry them a little.' So we'd sit down at NBC, and we'd be talking away, and he'd say, 'That'll worry them a little.' In the end, we didn't get a hell of a lot more money, but we did get more."

After fifty years in show business, Benjamin Sherman "Scatman" Crothers finally got his big break, or as he put it, "Fifty years, and now I'm an overnight success!" But he did not begrudge the lateness of his sudden rise from the ranks of character actors—whose faces fans know, but not their names—to national recognition. He was grateful for it. "Can you imagine for four years, fifty, sixty million people looking at you?" he said a few years later.

But he wasn't really surprised. "I've just kept busy in the

business and I just knew it, 'cause if you sow sparingly, you'll reap sparingly. But if you sow abundantly, you will reap abundantly."

He loved being on *Chico*. He volunteered to warm up the live studio audience before the taping of each show. He was delighted to walk around NBC's Burbank studios and sign autographs for excited fans. And there is no question that he enjoyed seeing the gravy train stop regularly for a change.

He and Helen moved to a new house in Van Nuys after he had been on the show for about a year. Helen still lives there. "We outgrew our other house," she says. "We'd been there twenty-one years. Donna had a big huge closet, and it was packed. She couldn't get another thing in it. Plus, our old neighborhood had changed; it just wasn't like it used to be. When we first moved in there, we went to sleep many a night with our door open. I used to leave Donna's tricycle, her little swimming pool, all of her toys, out in front. Nobody touched anything. Then these low-lifers started moving in. They would steal your hose, anything that wasn't hitched down."

In their search for a new home, Scatman and Helen had looked in Beverly Hills and Brentwood, but they'd decided those areas were too hilly. "We looked at this one three times before we decided," says Helen. "Some doctor used to own it. Scat finally said, 'Yeah, I like that house, let's take it.' "

It was a comparatively modest house in a middle-class section. Soon, Scatman and Helen knew all the neighbors, but this house would not be a neighborhood center as the old house had been.

"We had one big party the first year we moved here," says Helen. "Scat had been on *The Tonight Show*. They taped it earlier, and when they were finished taping, they all came over to our house, which was just a few minutes from the studio. The house was packed. I'd cooked all kinds of food, and everybody ate, and then when the show came on at eleven-thirty, everyone watched it."

'But after that, he said, 'Honey, let's not have any more

parties. You've worked so hard all these years. Let's just spend our time together.' "

They had been married nearly forty years, and still there were occasional times when a woman would try to drive a wedge between them. "I had a friend," says Helen, "who may have been jealous because we'd moved into this big, beautiful house. Anyhow, she had a friend of hers call and tell me that Scat was having an affair with her. When I told Scat, he said, 'Honey, that woman is all skin and bones. I don't want no woman with her bones sticking out.' Sometime later, the one who had called became ill with cancer. She must have had an attack of conscience, because she called and told me that Scat had never slept with that woman. She said, 'I have never known him to be anything but a gentleman.' I knew that."

When Helen and Scatman moved into the new house in Van Nuys, Donna, who had been living with them on Thirty-eighth and Cimmaron, did not move with them. It was time at last for her to live on her own.

"I was not ready for that move," she recalled. "I grew up here [in Los Angeles], all my friends are here. I was not ready for the Valley. The first time I went out there, I got lost. It's like a foreign world to me—still is." She visited frequently, and they visited her. They spoke on the telephone regularly. Parents and daughter continued to be protective—Donna says overprotective—of each other.

"Yeah, they're overprotective," she said in 1985, "but then I think we all are of each other. One day they came to visit. They left that evening, and they always called to tell me that they had gotten home all right. Well, this evening they didn't call and didn't call. I couldn't understand why they weren't home. They had stopped at a store or to eat or something, but I was so worried. So now I kind of appreciate where they're coming from. I still have to check in. Even from this house I have to check in—'I'm leaving and I'll be back at eight-thirty and I'll give you a call.' It's nice to know that they care."

Eventually, Helen got a Los Angeles telephone number so

the two could talk several times a days by phone without having to call long distance. Scatman and Helen understood that it was time for Donna to be on her own, and she, in turn, saw how happy they were in their new home. "They are really enjoying it out there," she said in 1985.

Scatman got Donna on *Chico and the Man* three or four times. For some years, he had urged her to get work as an extra and she had done some work in that area, although as she explains, "I'm too shy and too introverted to get in front of a camera and speak words. My God, I'd be tongue-tied.

"I was working at a factory, the graveyard shift at that. I think he did not like the fact that I was going there at midnight and working until seven or eight A.M., and then driving home half-asleep. He said, 'Be an extra. Go and get a portfolio and take it around to the casting places. It's easy money.' I tried it, and it worked. I got into it."

Donna was on a *Doris Day Show*. She did a beer commercial with old family friend Redd Foxx and appeared on *The Redd Foxx Show*. In one job, she was a fan at a night baseball game at the Coliseum. It was a cold night, and she nearly froze, for fifty-five dollars. Eventually, she said, "Daddy, I can't do this. It's too phony." Scatman understood.

The new house was only twelve minutes away from the Burbank Studios. Scatman would get up two hours before he was due there—8:00 A.M. Monday through Wednesday, 7:00 A.M. on Thursday and Friday. On most days, he was home by about 4:00 P.M., except on Friday, when the show was taped and he was done by 10:00 A.M., with plenty of time for a couple of rounds of golf with Albertson. Thursday was the hardest for Scatman and the rest of the cast. "That's camera-blocking day," he explained, "and to me that's the toughest day because you say a line and the guy in the booth says, 'Hold it right there.' " It was a schedule that had done in more than one actor half his age, but Scatman thrived on it.

Della Reese joined the cast of *Chico and the Man* in 1976, playing the part of Ed's landlady, Della Rogers. She was the only other character to be added who proved to be popular with the audience. Like Scatman, she was with the show to the end.

Scatman was popular on the *Chico* set. Producer James Komack had come to love Scatman, who frequently stopped by Komack's house on Sundays to play guitar and sing to his children. "Scatman has about 104 teeth," he told Gerry Nadel of *TV Guide* in early 1976, "any 80 of which are constantly blinding you. . . . He'll do dumb jokes—old, old horrible jokes—but he makes them *work*."

At the age of sixty-eight, Jack Albertson had been in show business nearly as long as Scatman and appreciated his professionalism, for Scatman never questioned what was asked of him. Albertson understood that the grueling schedule of a weekly television series was difficult for an older person and marveled at Scat's energy. He also enjoyed being around Scatman and had become one of Scatman's regular golfing partners. "Scat did the driving," says Helen, "Because Jack didn't see so good."

The show's star, Freddie Prinze, admired Scatman, too, and was grateful that Scatman often took it upon himself to help protect Prinze from the crowds of fans waiting for him outside the NBC studios. "We were pretty tight on the set," Scatman recalled, "but we didn't see each other outside of the show. He often said to me, 'Man, I'm never going to live to be as old as you,' and I'd say, 'You shouldn't talk that way. How do you know how long you're gonna live?' "

Sadly, Prinze would not live to be even twenty-five. *Chico* was in its fourth season, after three seasons as the top-rated show on television, when its young star began to show signs of severe emotional instability.

He seemed not to appreciate his good fortune in becoming a star so young and almost literally overnight. Friends reported that he acted as if it was all his due, and he was disappointed that there wasn't more. His attitude was, "Is that all there is?"

His 1975 marriage to Kathy Cochran, with whom he had a

son, lasted only about a year. He seemed to prefer living on the edge, and the company of young Hollywood comedians who were deeply involved with drugs. He was reported to take ten quaaludes a day, as well as three grams of cocaine. He didn't have to worry about getting drugs—they were all around him. Fans sent him pills and cocaine in the mail. The drugs made a deadly combination with his tendency to morbid depression and his fascination with guns.

He was obsessed by the legend of Lenny Bruce, whose recorded routines he knew by heart. Once, he went to the late comedian's home, took a leaf from a tree in the yard, and put it in his wallet.

Prinze was also fascinated by the assassination of President John F. Kennedy, who was killed when Prinze was only eight years old. He obtained copies of the news footage of that day in Dallas and played it over and over on his VCR—in slow motion.

In early January 1977, Prinze was arrested for driving under the influence of methaqualone. He was under medical treatment for depression, and he spoke of committing suicide. On the night of January 27, 1977, he spent a great deal of time on the telephone, calling his friends, talking about suicide. Of the many people he called, only Dusty Snyder, his business manager, caught the note of urgency in Prinze's voice, and went to his home to be with him. Snyder was present at 3:30 A.M. when Prinze shot himself in the head with his .32 automatic pistol. He died a few hours later at UCLA Medical Center.

Scatman recalled, "Jimmy Komack told me that Freddie had been talking about committing suicide for months, but I didn't know that. That Thursday [before his suicide] we were camera-blocking at the studio. I remember that was the night my episode on *Roots* was on, and I missed it because we were blocking. Freddie walks up and puts his arm around me and whispers in my ear, 'Scat, I think I'll kill myself.' And I said, 'Aw, come on, Freddie, don't talk that way, son. You're twenty-two years old, and you haven't begun to live, and you're just getting ready to make it big.' He said, 'I guess you're right.' I said, 'Don't you talk to your wife?' He said, 'Naw.' He said he tried, but they couldn't get together. So I said, 'Listen. Forget your wife and think about yourself. Because the Bible says self-preservation is the first law of nature.' He said, 'Yeah,' and that night he shot himself."

It was an act that was beyond Scatman's comprehension. Here was a kid who had made it at age twenty-two, who seemingly had everything to live for, and he had thrown it away. Scatman attended the funeral on January 31, but only because it was expected of him. He wasn't one for funerals. "I try to help people while they're living," he said in 1986. "A friend of mine passed away a week ago—one of the Step Brothers. I didn't go to the funeral. I don't go to funerals. The last funeral I went to was Freddie Prinze's, and that's because I had to. It was shocking [to learn of his death]. The minute I heard it on the news, in my heart I hated it. But then I was glad in my heart that I had told the boy the right thing. So then I said, 'Well, my conscience is clear.' "

In the late summer of 1990, both the television programs *Entertainment Tonight* and *Inside Edition* chose to recall the death of Prinze over thirteen years earlier and to ask again: why? But they offered no new information.

The comedian David Brenner, who had been a friend of Prinze's, continued to subscribe to the too-much-too-soon theory, saying that Prinze had got on a subway in the Bronx and stepped out of a Rolls-Royce in Beverly Hills.

Della Reese still felt it had been a tragic accident and that Prinze had been merely clowning around. Dusty Snyder, Prinze's agent at the time of his death, continued to feel that Prinze had a death wish, as did James Komack.

After Prinze's death, Komack hoped to be able to keep *Chico and the Man* on the air even without its young star, banking on the popularity of Jack Albertson and Scatman. To end the 1976–77 season, the writers explained Chico's absence by saying he had gone to Mexico. As the next season approached, a couple of the show's best writers left, but Komack hoped to keep the old audience and attract a new one with the introduction of Gabriel Melgar, a twelve-year-old Chicano whom

Scatman regarded as an adorable and brainy kid. Scatman was given second billing, after Albertson; Melgar was billed third. Della Reese remained part of the cast as Ed's landlady, and was given a peripatetic son played by the young comedian Franklyn Ajaye.

The television press were treated to a preview of the episode introducing Melgar as Raul at a screening in Chicago in August 1977. Ed (Albertston) and Louie (Scatman) return from a fishing trip in Mexico and discover a stowaway (Raul) curled up in the trunk of their car. He immediately makes himself comfortable in Ed's garage and charms Della. When Ed says he is going to turn Raul, whom he keeps calling "Chico" by mistake, over to immigration authorities, Raul retorts that he'll say he was forcibly taken for cheap labor.

Chico and the Man did not last long after the death of Freddie Prinze, however. "The show got too 'productive,' it lost its simplicity," Scatman said. He believed the show might have had a chance if Prinze's absence had been explained earlier. "The main problem was that they should have opened the new season with the reason for Chico being gone. They waited too long to do that. Also, we lost a few good writers. Hal Kanter was one. He was great."

After eighty-eight *Chico* shows, Scatman's longest run on television was over.

About eighteen months earlier, Scatman had suggested to Komack that the producer develop a spin-off from *Chico and the Man* as a starring vehicle for himself. Komack had gone along with the idea, although he worried about interfering with the good chemistry between the present cast and the *Chico* audience. During 1976, Scatman had spoken frequently to the TV press about the proposed pilot: "It's set in New Orleans," he told one source. "I own this club, and I have a niece or a granddaughter, I'm not sure which yet. It's about contrasts. She has an Angela Davis attitude and I'll say things like one line I wrote for the pilot. It goes, 'Look, honey, I was colored before you was ever black.'

"And because I own the club, I can sing and play guitar on the show, which is different from what I can do as Louie collecting the garbage on *Chico.* It will present my other talents, of which I have a few. There'll be nothing like it on TV, I'll guarantee."

No question that it was a timely idea, given the militant turn the black struggle had taken and the current generation gap between older, more moderate blacks and Young Turks like Angela Davis, an avowed communist who at the time was on the FBI's most-wanted list for assisting in an abortive California prison escape. Moreover, Scatman had proved his popularity with TV audiences and had the many talents of which he spoke. The pilot was not made during the run of *Chico,* and there had been no guarantee it ever would be made. However, Scatman was philosophical about it, saying, "What will be will be."

While Scatman missed the live audience before which he had performed in *Chico,* he had plenty to do after the show was canceled. In fact, since he had become a regular on *Chico,* he'd had as much work as he could handle.

Because of his schedule on *Chico,* he had done few performance dates, but in the summer, when the show was in reruns, he found the time to appear locally. In August 1975, he was on a bill at the Ice House with comedienne Julie McWhirter and Baum and Estin, a guitar and banjo act. Wrote the reviewer in the August 21, 1975, issue of *Variety,* "Minstrel Scatman Crothers and his guitar sit in for one of the most polished performances of recent memory at Pasadena showcase. Both urbane and modest, singer demonstrates his pro status as he ripples through collection of oldies, evokes anguish with 'Dead Man's Blues,' works to high plateau with insistent rhythm of 'Walk On, Nigger, Walk On' from 'Coonskin' film.

"Enunciation, timbre, emphasis, phrasing, modulation are superb, should serve as required study for younger performers who crowded Thursday night's opening. Eloquent tribute to his wife, 'Waitin' For My Baby,' holds universal appeal, and 35-

minute turn, including 'Biscuit Song,' 'Everything Will Be Okay,' medley of w.k. tunes, plus his own Scat singing on 'Ain't She Sweet,' is winner all the way around."

He also did a considerable amount of performing abroad, and traveled to Hong Kong, Manila, the Philippines, and Australia.

On television, in addition to guest shots on series such as *Petrocelli* and *Sanford and Son*, TV specials like the Jonathan Winters special *Two Hundred Years of Comedy*, and television movies like *Man on the Outside*, the two-hour pilot for the series *Griff*, starring Lorne Greene, that, oddly enough, did not air until eighteen months after the series was canceled, being a regular on the top-rated TV series had gained him entrée to the TV talk-show circuit. In 1975, he appeared three times on *The Dinah Shore Show*, once on *The Mike Douglas Show* when the guest host was Dyan Cannon, and was invited to appear ten times on *The Tonight Show*, although he didn't actually get on the show that often. As he pointed out to Johnny Carson one night when he finally did get on, "The last time I was on your show, or should I say the first time, I didn't get to do the number. Then I was on again and didn't get to do it. Then I was a standby once. Now this is the third time. Maybe we could do 'The Biscuit Song' this time." He'd been doing that song for forty-odd years. His act didn't change, just as he didn't.

Scatman also appeared on *The David Steinberg Show*, and on Sammy Davis's short-lived talk show *Sammy and Company*. He guested on *The Rich Little Show*, *Celebrity Sweepstakes*, and the series *Lohman and Barkley*.

That same year, Scatman filmed the highest-rated miniseries in the history of TV, *Roots*, which was broadcast in 1976 and nominated for three dozen Emmys. In the miniseries, based on writer Alex Haley's best-selling book of the same title, Scatman played the cockfighter Mingo.

According to Scatman, the producers had wanted him for another part originally. He would not say which part, but it was probably the role of Chicken George, which was played by Cleavon Little. At that time, Scatman's work on *Chico and the*

Man precluded his taking a role that involved more than a couple days' shooting. "They worked around my schedule on *Chico*," he said. He had no idea how successful the miniseries would be but enjoyed the work he did on it.

That same year, Steve Tisherman joined the Don Schwartz agency as a specialist in voice-overs. He took on Scatman's cartoon-voice representation. "I think the first job I got him was *Banjo the Woodpile Cat*," says Tisherman.

Scatman did the voice of Crazylegs in the animated feature for television created by a group of disgruntled cartoonists who had left Disney. "They thought a lot of him," says Tisherman. "It was very well received, and they certainly thought he helped present that show very beautifully. I believe it was nominated for an award."

Scatman was one of Tisherman's more unusual clients. "I remember making a voice-over tape. The [Schwartz] agency had no voice-over business, and I wanted a tape to show what our clients could do. I picked out copy for everybody to come in and read at the studio. With him, I couldn't find anything. So I just said, 'Scat, get in front of the microphone and lay some things down.' He talked for about four minutes. He did a little character, he went into a little song, but mostly he just talked about 'What am I doing here?' It didn't make sense from a copy standpoint, but with him it didn't have to. I needed a thirty-second clip, so he talked and I cut a thirty-second clip representative of what he could possibly do in commercials, and it worked beautifully."

Scatman got little standard commercial voice-over work. "He did a few noncartoon voice-overs, but not many," says Tisherman. "Because his style was so specific, they had to want to buy him as a representative of their product, not just 'get me a black actor to represent this product.'

"It was the way he did things—his flair—which to a lot of advertisers was sort of difficult for them to put into a vehicle that could work. That's why he didn't work so much on or off camera in commercials. If *Chico* had still been on, or if his other shows were still on the air—the longer he would have been on a network show going into homes every week, the more chance he would have found something commercially, because they would have created based on the success of him in that show."

But Scatman was often specifically requested for cartoon work. "Most people knew him, and he was certainly an original," says Tisherman. "There was nobody who could do what he could do, so if you were creating an animated situation with a character that remotely required something like him, your mind almost couldn't think of anybody else to use. He was just so genuine. He played himself—not to demean him as an actor, because he had proved he could act—but in the animation area, he played his outrageous self, which worked so well."

In 1977, in addition to making the rounds of the talk shows, Scatman was a judge on *The Gong Show*, did a guest spot on *Starsky and Hutch*, participated in the *Dean Martin Roast for Ted Knight* special, and appeared in the ABC-TV Movie of the Week, *Undercover Elephant*.

During the years 1975 and 1976, as well as a good part of 1977, Scatman did all this extra TV work on top of a full season on *Chico*, which was quite a schedule for a man in his middle sixties to maintain. His daughter, Donna, recalls, "He was so tired all the time." But Scatman was far too realistic about the vagaries of the entertainment business not to exploit his exposure on *Chico* for all it was worth, only too aware that fame could depart as swiftly as it arrived. He told both his wife and daughter that he was fixing it so they would never have to worry about money again.

During the run of *Chico*, Scatman also continued to accept as many film offers as he could. His exposure on *Chico* had done wonders for his film career, and he was constantly in demand for movies during the run of the show.

In 1975, he appeared in *Friday Foster*, produced and directed by Arthur Marks, who also wrote the story. It was an unsuccessful attempt to change Pam Grier's image from that of a supermama type, which she had played in such films as *Coffy* (1973) and *Foxy Brown* (1974) and which, like the black buck characters played by Jim Brown, was fast going out of style. In this American International Pictures film, Grier played a fashion photographer who uncovered and destroyed a white group bent on assassinating black leaders. Co-starring were Yaphet Kotto as Grier's buddy, Eartha Kitt as an eccentric designer, Carl Weathers as a villain, and Godfrey Cambridge as an effeminate designer. Film historian Donald Bogle assesses it as an average made-for TV-type movie that probably plays better on TV than it did originally in the theaters.

Also released in 1975 by Columbia Pictures was *The Fortune*, starring Warren Beatty and Jack Nicholson, a slapstick farce set in the 1920s about a greedy sheik (Beatty) and a low-lifer (Nicholson) who plot to kill heiress Stockard Channing. Mike Nichols directed the film, which also featured Dub Taylor, Richard B. Shull, Ian Wolfe, and Florence Stanley. Scatman played a fisherman.

The most controversial picture Scatman was in that year was *Coonskin,* a part-animated, part live-action cartoon update of the old Uncle Remus stories. Set in an urban ghetto, it focuses on three blacks, Brother Rabbit, Brother Bear, and Preacher, who arrive in Harlem from the country, are appalled at how the mob has overrun the ghetto, and determine to clean it up, only to end up controlling the drug, prostitution, and gambling trades themselves.

Written and directed by Ralph Bakshi, whose earlier animated films, *Fritz the Cat* and *Heavy Traffic,* were striking visions of harsh ghetto life (Bakshi had grown up in the Bedford-Stuyvesant section of Brooklyn), *Coonskin* starred singer Barry White as Brother Bear, Philip Michael Thomas as Brother Rabbit, and Charles Gordone, the black playwright and author of *No Place to Be Somebody,* as the Preacher. Scatman played Pappy and Old Man Bone. (According to Steve Tisherman, animators generally liked to get two characters for the price of one.)

The film opens with two black convicts, Philip Michael Thomas and Scatman, waiting in a prison yard for an escape car to appear. Scatman fills in the time by telling his young friend a story, which is a modernized version of an Uncle Remus tale.

Scatman also sang the title song, "Walk On, Nigger, Walk On," which he wrote with Bakshi, part of which went like this:

I'm a minstrel man
I'm a cleaning man
I'm the shoeshine man
I'm the coal man. . . .
I'm a nigger man.
Watch me dance! . . .
I got the Devil in me
It was The Man you see
He put that Devil in me. . . .
Walk on, Nigger, walk on.

The film was given a special screening at the Museum of Modern Art before its official release, after which all hell broke loose. Civil-rights organizations like CORE (Congress of Racial Equality) criticized it as full of demeaning stereotypes. According to Elaine Parker, the chairperson of CORE's Harlem branch, "It depicts blacks as slaves, hustlers, and whores. It is . . . very insulting." Whereupon, CORE launched a campaign to prevent the movie's distribution.

Paramount Pictures, which was originally to distribute the film, backed out. An independent company, Bryanston, picked up the distribution rights, hoping, no doubt, that the pre-release publicity would boost ticket sales.

When the film finally premiered in New York, pickets lined the streets outside the theaters where it was playing. *The New York Times* devoted a full-page article to it. But soon the controversy died down, and the film died with it.

Scatman didn't see what all the fuss was about. "When that movie opened in New York, the paper said that the song got a standing ovation—even though by mid-show they almost had a riot on their hands," he told Linda Olsen of *Players*. "I appeared at the Troubadour with Chick Corea and I opened with that song. Standing room only. Redd Foxx used to come up and do a few numbers. We did 'All of Me' there."

Black audiences did not find *Coonskin* particularly offensive, accustomed as they already were to "blaxploitation" films whose plots were not all that different from that of *Coonskin*. Black and white audiences did not find it especially entertaining, for while some of the animated sections contained dazzling effects, the plot line was weak, and the animated and live sections were not well integrated. In the end, the pre-release hoopla over *Coonskin* proved to be much ado about nothing.

The most important role Scatman had in the middle 1970s was that of Turkle, the sweetly lecherous, drunken, and beleaguered orderly in *One Flew Over the Cuckoo's Nest,* starring Jack Nicholson. Based on a 1962 novel by Ken Kesey about life in a mental institution, and directed by Milos Forman, it was a harrowing comedy-melodrama that captured the essence of 1960s paranoia.

Originally, Scatman's part was larger than it was in the finished product, in which his character's main function was to permit the wild party that led to the film's tragic finale. It represents some of the finest acting in his career, for he did not play himself. There was one scene that he felt especially good about that was cut. "I did that scene, and quite a few people started applauding," he recalled. "Milos Forman [the director] ran and grabbed me and hugged me and said, 'Scat, that was beautiful, you're gonna be in all my movies,' and then he left the scene on the cutting-room floor." Scatman's one memorable line in the scenes of his that were retained was, "You crazy mumpa fumpas, you'll make me lose my job!" There were many other memorable lines in the film, which won Academy Awards for Best Picture, Director, Actor, Actress, and Screenplay.

The movie was filmed in Salem, Oregon. When he wasn't needed on camera, Scatman spent his time visiting local schools and hospitals. At one school, a retarded boy came to him timidly, wanting to tell him he liked him in *Hong Kong Phooey.* But he couldn't get the words out. Sensing the boy's frustration, Scatman asked him, "Would you pour me a drink?" Against his teacher's better judgment, the boy grabbed a pitcher and poured Scatman a glass of water, not spilling a drop. "Oh my," Scatman said. "No one pours that water like you, son. Pour me some more!" The boy beamed.

In 1976, Scatman appeared with John Wayne and Hugh O'Brian, with whom he hadn't worked since *Meet Me at the Fair,* in *The Shootist* for Paramount. Also appearing in the film were Lauren Bacall, James Stewart, Ron Howard, Richard Boone, Harry Morgan, and a host of other stars. "That was [Wayne's] last picture," Scatman recalled. "He was a beautiful man." Scatman played a character named Moses (as he had in *Bloody Mama*), a stable owner.

Also in 1976 he appeared in *Silver Streak* with Richard Pryor and Gene Wilder. "In that one," said Scatman, whose character was named Ralston, "I play a Pullman porter who saves everybody's lives. The only thing that bothered me about that film was hanging off the train. It was going too fast for my liking. But they told me to just hang on tight, and I said, 'Don't worry, you're gonna have to unglue me.' "

Film historian Donald Bogle characterized Scatman's work as "performing some comic coon antics that are a pure throwback to the films of the 1930s," but what better actor to turn in such a performance in what was intended to be a thirties-type mystery-comedy than a man who remembered how it was done? Scatman had no objection to playing a porter and was proud of his work in the film, just as he continued to be proud of the work he had done earlier in his career.

"I don't pay them any mind," he said about those who called him an Uncle Tom. "Feel sorry for them, though. Especially now. It's heaven for the young black man today. The door is open, all he's got to do is walk through it. He should use the energy he's burning up on being angry to qualify himself for whatever he wants to do. Just because I play the part of a gangster doesn't mean I am one. Acting is just that—acting. And these youngsters should stop paying attention to what other folks are doing and spend that time working on developing their own wants."

Scatman, a truly free man, felt no need for posturing or for proving himself. He'd known who he was since he was in his teens.

CHAPTER 8

STILL GOING STRONG

WITH THE CANCELLATION OF *Chico and the Man,* Scatman hoped for the go-ahead on the long-talked-about pilot about a New Orleans club owner, which he thought should be called *Way Down Yonder.* He even had the title song written, about the Club Gumbo:

Everybody's goin' down to Club Gumbo
Club Gumbo, Club Gumbo
Way down yonder in New Orleans
It's the land of my dreams
Beautiful Creole queens
You know what it means
It's the place to go, to see a good show
Club Gumbo, Club Gumbo, Club Gumbo
Way down yonder in New Orleans
Yeah!

Several other black situation comedies were on TV at the time and doing well, among them *Good Times.* Scatman thought his show would fit right in. To remind NBC that he was still available, he even wrote a little ditty and sent it to Fred Silverman, the new man in charge of programming at NBC: "Everybody's been waitin' for you, Fred/'Cause NBC has been dead/ I'm glad that you have arrived/To make NBC come alive." But the pilot never materialized.

Fortunately, he did get another cartoon-voice job with the new Hanna-Barbera series *The Skatebirds,* which featured the voice of Mickey Dolenz of The Monkees and which included not only animated segments but also live-action segments, though these involved a different cast.

At sixty-seven, Scatman was of an age to start thinking about retirement and spending most of his time playing golf. But he did not feel he was in a position to do so financially. The steady pay he'd received for a few years on *Chico and the Man,* and whatever else he'd earned doing films and TV specials, had not enabled him to build up what he considered a proper nest egg for himself and Helen, not to mention Helen and Donna after he was gone.

Besides, Scatman loved to perform and could not imagine life without performing. He now had an opportunity to get back into club work, which he had rarely been able to do during his years on *Chico* because of the demands of a weekly TV series. Among his first appearances with a new trio were at the Trojan Horse in Seattle and at San Diego's Mexican-American Festival of Stars.

Teddy Edwards recalls that the last time they actually performed together was on a video called *America's Music,* produced by Skylark Productions. "They had a lot of great artists—B.B. King, Linda Hopkins, Ruth Brown, Billy Eckstine. They did a series of about twenty of them, and I think Scatman was either on the blues or the rhythm-and-blues segment."

Scatman was delighted to be considered in the pantheon of America's great musicians. In his day, he felt he had been, although his television and film work had eclipsed his musical career.

He also accepted as many invitations as came his way to appear in celebrity golf tournaments, for they gave him an opportunity to perform as well as to play golf. "He wasn't what you'd call [a] good golfer," says Phil Harris, who did the celebrity tournament tour along with Scatman. "But what the hell, there's a lot of duffers out there. Everybody loved him and wanted him to play. Most of the places he would go—and I would go—is because we'd entertain, too. They'd put on a show. In the Crosby tournament, the clambake was as famous as the golf tournament. You take Doug Sanders's tournament or Roy Clark's, we'd all go in, and they'd have more talent than they knew what to do with.

"You didn't have to perform, but you actually wanted to, because you were all friends. So you'd go on and do your little number, whatever it was. That's why they called the Crosby thing a clambake, because nothing was ever written out; it was kind of like a jam session. Scatman used to love to do that, and he had more tournaments than he knew what to do with because everybody wanted him. He was very generous with his time."

Asked by a reporter for the *San Diego Evening Tribune* about his golf game in the summer of 1977, Scatman said, "I've been playing in so many tournaments that sometimes I think I'm on tour. But I tell you, if I was on tour, I'd be the only guy on tour and on welfare."

The late Don Schwartz recalled that both he and Scatman were interested in exploiting Scatman's multiple talents as an entertainer. Schwartz firmly believed that Scatman could carry off a one-man show on Broadway and urged his best client to develop that type of routine. Scatman liked the idea of a one-man show, although he was resistant to actually going to Broadway.

"A friend and I created a show around his life," said Schwartz. "He comes out talking about how he danced as a kid and then a little kid comes out of the shadows and dances with him. In another section, a group is singing 'One Man Show,' and he stops and says, 'That's my number. I'm the one-man show.' This was a great number."

Schwartz recalled that they tried it out on *The Tonight Show* on New Year's Eve when Orson Bean was the host: "It was the first time I ever saw Scat have any fear and get nervous. What happened was that Doc Severinsen's band thought that Scat had his typical material, but this was a difficult, scored thing—Broadway scored. And, Scat had never heard the arrangement, and Doc didn't know it. Doc figured he'd give Scat five minutes to rehearse. Finally, I got to Doc, and I said, 'Scat's nervous; he's never done this.' So then Doc realized it, and they rehearsed it, and they only had about ten minutes to rehearse a very complicated Broadway-type show tune. That was the only time I'd ever seen him nervous. They'd had a few drinks backstage, and I think that didn't help either. The timing was a little slow on the number; he messed up the lyrics a little bit. But nobody else noticed it, and it went over. Orson Bean said, 'That's a Broadway show-stopper; it's a real hit.' Everybody said it was. But we couldn't get the money at the time. He was sort of interested, and then things really started happening for him and he never really wanted to go back [to the stage].'

Schwartz's biggest regret was that he never got Scatman to agree to try Broadway. "If that man had appeared on Broadway, he could have been a worldwide name. He could have been a big star in the nature of a Mae West or a Will Rogers. Maybe not quite that big, but he could have been big because he had the ability to capture an audience, and New York would have gone crazy over him."

Failing to get Scatman to New York, Schwartz turned to Las Vegas. "They wanted him to play the lounge, and I think he did it once. Then we decided we were going to hold out for the opening of somebody else's show. They never realized how good he could have been for Vegas, because the families would have loved him. And the gamblers would have loved him, too. The gamblers love people like him, because he was so blunt and straightforward."

Undaunted, Scatman and his agent pursued the idea of a Broadway-type revue titled *The Scatman Crothers Show*. Fletcher Smith says he put the show together. Musicians included drummer Bruno Carr and trumpet player Clora Bryant; Kandi Moore and Sandi Humphries were backup singers.

"Scat called me," says Clora Byrant, "and I joined the revue as both a singer and a musician. I sang backup for him, and then I had my own spot where I played and did my imitation of Louis Armstrong."

Clora Bryant had not worked with Scatman since the 1950s. In the interim, she had played behind Billie Holiday and Josephine Baker, with all the "girl bands" such as the Sweethearts, the Darlings, and the Queens of Swing, which had been the first all-female jazz group on television in the 1950s, and had gone back to college to get her B.A. "I was on the road a lot," she says, "and I had lived in Canada and New York and Chicago, so we had kind of lost touch. It was fun to get back together with Scat." In the summer of 1978, they toured for six weeks, performing at the Parisian Room in Los Angeles, at the White House club in Newport Beach, and at the Playboy Club in Dallas, among other venues.

The July 31, 1978, *Variety* review of the show at the Parisian Room was glowing: "For fans who remember him from earlier years, the only thing missing from Scatman Crothers' new act is the nonsense syllables which, among other benefits, spawned his nickname. Obviously, he wanted to do something different, something built on a mesh of talents rather than a flood of vocal acrobatics. It worked fine. Crothers proved once again that he can shift his multifaceted talent in a lot of directions, including emphasis on comedy laced with lighthearted songs, which is his current fare.

"What he was after became obvious as soon as he bounded onto the stage with a trash barrel as a reminder of his late role in *Chico and the Man.*

" 'Just remember,' he joshed, 'that I'll empty anybody's can.' "

"Then came the comic tunes: 'That Old Gang of Mine,' with fresh lyrics about the Parisian Room clientele and other contemporaries: 'The Mean Dog Blues'; 'Some of My Best Friends Are Shoes'; and of course 'The Biscuit Man' (I'm the only one who can take a biscuit apart and put it back together the way it was.')

"Crothers is an admitted 68, and, as he observed in the tune he opened and closed with, 'still going strong.' He is, indeed. The vigor and cheerful showmanship remain, and the now slightly heavier gravel enhances his timbre ideally for the kind of insouciant humor he sells."

"Add a fine combo, a femme singing trio and an opening act featuring Clora Bryant's hot jazz trumpet, and he has assembled a show with all the elements of a smash."

Meanwhile, Scatman continued to take whatever film roles were offered of which he could approve. He appeared in two films released in 1978—*The Cheap Detective* and *Mean Dog Blues*. *The Cheap Detective*, written by Neil Simon, starred Peter Falk as a wacky Bogart-type detective running around San Francisco. Scatman played Tinker, a piano player reminiscent of Sam in *Casablanca*; in a very funny bit, Falk almost breaks his fingers for playing the song "Jeepers Creepers." It is possible that this role led to Scatman's being chosen to play the piano player in the 1983 TV series *Casablanca*.

Mean Dog Blues was a prisoner-on-the-run picture starring Gregg Henry, Kay Lenz, and George Kennedy. Scatman, who was billed fourth, played the character named Mudcat. An American International Pictures release, it was a Bing Crosby Productions film.

Scatman's TV work in 1978 included guest shots on the series *Welcome Back, Kotter*, produced by James Komack, *Flying High*, *Charlie's Angels*, *The Love Boat*, *Vegas*, and *Laugh Olympics*. He also appeared on *The Jim Nabors Show*, *The Tonight Show*, and *The Dinah Shore Show*, and several TV specials: *Comedy Shop*, *NBC 25-Year Salute to the Wonderful World of Disney*, *Puppy's Great Adventure*, *Opening Night Variety*, and *The Harlem Globetrotters*.

In 1979, he appeared on the series *Make Me Laugh*, *The Incredible Hulk*, and again on *Vegas*. He also appeared on *The Tonight Show* again. "Why do you always put Negroes on last?" he wanted to know after he came on with an energetic number. "I get short of breath and can't talk." "Well, Scat," was the rejoinder, "just think if people get up early, you'll be on first."

He'd brought a letter from Fred Silverman thanking him for the song he'd written. In it, Silverman said that there had been a lot of material written about him lately, but that none of it had been original or as appreciative as his song. Unfortunately, the letter did not persuade Silverman to try Scatman's series.

Scatman played the character Sam in the film *Scavenger Hunt,* released in 1979, an all-star comedy featuring Richard Benjamin, Ruth Gordon, Dyan Cannon, Cloris Leachman, James Coco, and others, which was directed by Michael Schultz, the black director who had first made a name for himself with *Car Wash.* In the film, Vincent Price plays a millionaire who includes in his will a scavenger hunt; the person who finds the most items on the list gets his money. Scatman filmed one scene at the Huntington, California, library, and another, where he steals a suit of armor, at the San Diego Zoo. He also sang a song, written by Carol Connors and Billy Goldenberg, titled "There's Enough for Everyone."

In the summer, he took *The Scatman Crothers Show* to the Old New Yorker in North Hollywood, among other venues.

For most of 1979, however, Scatman was busy filming *The Shining,* perhaps his most difficult film to date but also a film in which he did some of his best work.

The Warner Bros. film was based on a novel by horror writer Stephen King, a gothic tale about a writer who takes his wife and child to spend the winter in an isolated, snowbound, haunted hotel in Colorado where he has taken a job as the caretaker. While there, the writer, played by Jack Nicholson, tries to kill his wife, played by Shelley Duvall, to the horror of their young son, played by Danny Lloyd. A kindly old cook with extrasensory powers (a gift he calls "the shining") recognizes that the young boy also possesses the gift, and eventually rescues mother and son.

Scatman read the Stephen King novel long before there was talk of a movie. As he told it, he was in Houston at the Houston Open Golf Tournament when someone there told him he'd just read a book by Stephen King who must have been thinking about Scatman when he created the cook, Dick Halloran.

When the movie *The Shining* was in the planning stages, director Stanley Kubrick wanted Halloran to be played by the veteran character actor Slim Pickens, with whom he had worked previously. But according to Don Schwartz, Pickens didn't want to do the film because he found Kubrick difficult to work with. Indeed, Kubrick, whose previous films had included *Dr. Strangelove, 2001: A Space Odyssey,* and *Paths of Glory,* was well known in the industry as the most perfectionist director in the business.

"Slim Pickens's agent was a friend of mine," said Schwartz, "which is how I found out about the part. I read it, and it was as if it was written for Scat. I told my agent friend that I was going to try to get it for Scat. I fought for one year to get that part. We called Jack Nicholson in New York, who was Scat's friend, to see if he could influence Kubrick. Then one day a representative of Kubrick's called and asked, 'Well, what will he do it for?' "

According to Scatman, the next time he saw Nicholson, the younger actor said, "Well, ol' buddy, we're about to do our fourth classic together." Scatman always said that it was Nicholson who got him the part.

Scatman had never heard of Stanley Kubrick. He recalled, 'I told a friend of mine at NBC, Henry Harris, 'Well, old buddy, I'm getting ready to go to London for the first time to do a movie.' He says, 'Who's directing?' and like a dumb cluck I say, 'I think the guy's name is Stan or Stanley.'

"He says, 'Kubrick? Man, don't you know you're going to be working with one of the world's greatest directors?' I said, 'No, but I know it now.'

"I'd never seen any of his work until I saw the screening in New York. But he is a phenomenal man, yes sir."

Most of the filming was done in England, and because of Kubrick's perfectionism, it took months and months to complete. Scatman was there in the spring of 1978, and celebrated his sixty-eighth birthday there. Jack Nicholson sent him a card with a message that parodied one of the tunes Scatman was always composing: "It ain't too late/To be great/At sixty-eight."

Scatman was back in London in the fall, and for the better part of 1979. For the first time in forty-three years, he and

Helen did not spend Christmas together. "Scatman spent the better part of two years over there,"said Don Schwartz, "doing nothing most of the time. Kubrick wanted him to stay over there so in case Kubrick called, he was there. He worked an awfully long time, and he lost a lot of money because of it. We wanted to do it so badly that we didn't get the kind of money we should have gotten, and then Scat had to turn down some great offers for much bigger money.

"Scat was offered two series. He was offered a lead in a series with that little short actor from *Wild Wild West* who had worked with Steve Ross—Marty Allen. They wanted him to fly into Chicago and do a big lead in one of his hour shows. He was offered the part of the trainer in *The Main Event*. But Kubrick said, 'No, he can't do it.' So Scat just sat there and cried. His wife told me he would call her and cry because he missed her so much and he was so lonely."

"It was terrible being apart so long," says Helen, "but I couldn't go over there and stay with him. Donna was here, and I had that big house and all those dogs to take care of. Plus, I had such bad arthritis, especially in my back.

"He was over in London for nine months, and he called me every day, without fail. Just before Thanksgiving, I went over there and stayed two weeks. The arthritis in my back was so bad that they had to take me out to the plane in a wheelchair. On the plane, they had to give me three or four seats across, and lots of pillows so I could lie down comfortably. Then, when I got over there, it was so rainy and cold. But it was worth it to see Scat. I stayed two weeks. We took the boat train to Paris one weekend. It was like a second honeymoon."

Schwartz also spent some time in London with Scatman. "We were staying at one of those little converted brownstones, a very popular hotel in Kensington," he recalled. "The rooms were very small, and I remember him joking that he had to back into the loo. Later on, I got his room because my room was so small. It was very hard to find hotel rooms at that time; London was very busy. They put me up in another hotel, and then he wanted to move out to the country nearer the studio, so I took his room, and he was right about the loo. He also said he was tired of telephones that sounded like birds—and they did, they went tweet, tweet.

"He hadn't lost his sense of humor, but he was very lonely and bored. He wasn't the type to pick up a book and read it. He had to play golf or sing. So I tried to get him some work. Actually, that's why I was over there, to get him some work.

"The hotel had a basement lounge, and I had a meeting with some agents there. I told them, 'You can't appreciate what an entertainer he is until you hear him sing.' He had his little guitar as always, and I asked him if he'd sing something. Well, he launched into one of his little routines, and, oh God, those old fogies were in a state of shock. The people who were sitting around in the lounge just loved it, but the agents were in absolute shock. Later on, they told him that they had just never seen anybody do anything like that. People just didn't do that sort of thing in public. They didn't want to represent him because they thought he was crude. They never said the word, but they intimated that what he had done in this little barlike place was not what was done in England."

Scatman, however, did get to perform once on a London stage. While he was there filming *The Shining* in May 1978, Diana Ross appeared at the London Palladium. Scatman and Jack Nicholson went to see her show, and right in the middle Ross announced, "I've got to stop the show because I see a couple of dear friends from America in the audience." She introduced Nicholson first, and he took a bow. Then she said, 'There's another gent with Jack who was with me in my first big movie, *Lady Sings the Blues*. He played the part of Big Ben. Scatman, come on up here and do a number.'

Scatman said to Ross's director, "Gil, let's do 'The Best Things in Life Are Free' in the key of C. I want an eight-bar intro and I'll do a couple of choruses with two or three tags on the second chorus and I'll kick it off, one-two-three."

He had a great time. "It was tremendous, man. I had a ball. So now I can tell the cats, 'I played the Palladium.' "

On the set of *The Shining*, Kubrick was being his usual detail-oriented self, ordering take after take on every scene. Scatman recalled the scene in which the viewer is first introduced to the hotel kitchen, a mammoth room that figures prominently in the building of suspense in the film. "He's a perfectionist and a genius," said Scatman. "Would you believe one day we did eighty-five takes on that minute-and-a-half scene? *Eighty-five takes!*

"Remember the scene when I go walking in the snow to the hotel? That was about forty takes. No dialogue, forty takes. One day I says to him, 'What was wrong that time, Stanley?' He says, 'You walked a little bit too far left.' I says, 'Okay, I'll try to walk a little bit to the right next time.' "

In Stephen King's novel, the cook is the hero who rescues the boy and his mother. But in the screenplay, which Stanley Kubrick wrote, the cook arrives at the resort for the rescue only to get a fatal ax blow in the chest from the maniacal Nicholson. Said Scatman, "I came back, trying to do the right thing and save the kid and his mother. But Stanley had me killed off. I guess he just said, 'Well, we'll just kill this nigger.' But hell, the money is the same."

The scene in which Nicholson kills him was another that Kubrick insisted be shot over and over again. No stunt man stood in for him, and Nicholson wielded a real ax. "I don't know why Stanley couldn't do it in one swing," Scatman said in 1985. "But he's such a perfectionist. Anyway, every time Jack would knock me clear across the floor. I used to tell Jack, 'Don't go crazy with that ax. And all the while the prop men were assuring me it couldn't go through my padding.

"Somebody said something about me being too old to fall down that many times, and Nicholson jumps in and says, 'Who says my man's too old to fall down? Why, he can fall down 50 or 60 times if he has to.'

"I wound up having to go to a chiropractor I was hurting so bad. My arms and elbows and neck and head got kind of beat up.

"The dialogue coach and the executive producer said, 'You've been over here a long time but when you win the Oscar you'll forget all about that.' I said, 'I don't have to win it. I'll be happy just to be nominated. I'll be happy just to have worked in the picture.' "

True to character, Scatman never blamed Kubrick for his discomfort. Asked about Kubrick by an interviewer for the *Philadelphia Evening Bulletin* in 1980, he responded, "Stan? Why, Stan is an ex-drummer. I wouldn't fight with no ex-drummer! I heard about the stuff that went on and what he and Jack were calling each other. But I can't comment on that. I was only on the set when I was working and nothing happened when I was working."

In fact, he wrote one of his songs—he called them his little gifts—for Kubrick called "Stanley (Does It All)."

> There's a man, lives in London town
> Makes movies, he's world renowned
> Yes he's really got the fame
> Stanley Kubrick is his name
> He does it all, he does it all
> I'm telling y'all, he does it all
> He's a writer, he directs
> He produces his projects
> He's the man behind the lens
> And Stanley always wins
> He's a man who looks ahead
> Can make you think he'll raise the dead
> Edison cuts all his flicks
> He's a genius with his tricks
> He does it all, he does it all
> Stanley does it all.

"His daughter over in England made a documentary of the filming of the movie," said Scat. "She said to me, 'Now when I interview you, Scatman, you will have to do the number that you have written for my father.' So it's in that documentary."

When Scatman saw the finished movie, however, he was more than a little disappointed that much of his best work wound up on the cutting-room floor. He was not nominated for an Academy Award. Said Don Schwartz, "He could have been nominated for an Oscar for *The Shining* if the picture hadn't been disliked, because everyone thought his performance in it was brilliant. Many critics said that he deserved to be nominated for an Oscar."

He did, however, get the Best Supporting Actor Award from the Academy of Science Fiction and Horror Films. "You know who I thought was going to win that year?" said Scatman. "Billy Dee Williams. I was just glad to be nominated. When they said *me*, I said, '*Whaaaat*?'" He also received an NAACP Image Award for his work as a supporting actor in the film.

He was not bitter—not about *The Shining* or about anything else. Said Don Schwartz, "He always said that what will be will be and in God we trust. If it happened, it happened; if it didn't, it didn't. He never tried to make a big case because something failed or didn't succeed in the way he had hoped."

Because of the length of time it took Stanley Kubrick to film *The Shining*, Scatman filmed *Bronco Billy* with Clint Eastwood in the interim. Like *The Shining*, *Bronco Billy* was a Warner Bros. film; Kubrick had to let him off to do it. He played Doc Lynch, the emcee for Bronco Billy's Wild West Show, and, after his role in *The King of Marvin Gardens*, it was his favorite. It was a big part, and he was featured throughout the film. Critics described his performance as "delightful."

Scatman thought a great deal of Clint Eastwood and enjoyed working with him. "Oh, that was great, great," he said of the experience. "We did it in seven weeks in Boise, Idaho. Clint doesn't like many takes. After eight months with Kubrick, I kept saying, 'Clint, are you sure that's all right?' We would do a couple, maybe three takes and I would go, 'Is that it?' 'Yes,' he would say. 'You're *not* working with Stanley now.'"

Of Eastwood, Scatman said, 'The man is so professional and so personable it's hard to believe. I've always wanted to work with him because I love his films and I know he really digs jazz. Well, it's been a joy."

As was his custom, he composed a song about Eastwood,

which he titled "Talkin' About a Man," to a country-style
tune:

>I'm talkin' about a man you see on the screen
>I'm talkin' about a man tall, lanky and lean
>I'm talkin' about a man who's oh! so good
>Talkin' 'about a man named Clint Eastwood
>I'm talkin' about a man that's humble and kind
>I'm talkin' 'bout a man with a beautiful mind
>His latest picture is Bronco Billy
>Made for every girl and little Willie
>You'll see him soon
>Some time in June
>No one gets killed
>They all get thrilled
>He's the roughest, toughest hombre
>The fastest draw with a lotta appall
>Bronco Billy is the most outrageous of 'em all
>It's superb entertainment that's really up to par
>You gonna love Clint Eastwood, cause he is a star
>Take it from me and go see
>It's rated P.G.
>Bronco Billy I'm sure is gonna make histor-y.

Scatman actually recorded a jazz version of the song, backed by
a star-studded group of his musician friends, among them Herb
Ellis on guitar, Jake Hannah on drums, Al Jackson on bass, Sid
Paige on violin, and Ross Tompkins (of *The Tonight Show* orchestra) on piano. He produced the record himself and had plans to
include the song on an album, which never materialized.

Both *Bronco Billy* and *The Shining* were in release at the
same time, a first for Scatman. The advantage for Warner Bros.
was that they could send Scatman out to do publicity for both
films. Helen and his publicist, Jerry Zelinka, accompanied him
on a brief publicity tour in the late spring and summer of 1980.

Scatman and his small entourage went first to New York for
that city's premiere of *The Shining*. Don Schwartz was there as

well. "It was his seventieth birthday," said Schwartz, "and they got a little party together for him at Joe Allen's, I believe, or one of those clubs on Forty-sixth Street. But it was a holiday weekend, and people were busy. I was very sick with pancreatitis at the time, but I was taking phone calls at the hotel from people like Gene Kelly who said they couldn't make it. But they went ahead with the party, and the people at the club asked Scat to perform. I'm telling you, that audience went crazy. The Warner Bros. people couldn't believe it. I knew that this man could take Broadway."

Jack Nicholson, whose trademark was sunglasses, as was Scatman's, presented him with a pair of white-framed, mirror-lensed Charles Jourdan wraparound sunglasses, and Scatman was delighted to wear them.

From New York, they continued on to Baltimore, where Scatman made the rounds of the radio stations singing his song about Clint Eastwood, those he wrote for Helen, "Mean Dog Blues," and others. The finish on his four-string Martin guitar was worn through, but Scatman had no intention of replacing it. He called it his baby, and took it everywhere. Once, as he boarded a plane, he was informed that he could not take it on with him. He protested. Fortunately, the pilot happened by. "Scatman," he said, "You just give it to me, and I'll keep it in the cockpit. And if this ever happens to you again, you just tell them to see the captain."

The promotional tour continued in the Midwest. In Detroit, he visited the offices of the *Detroit News* for pictures and an interview. Staff writer Jim McFarlin was struck by his winning manner: "Preparing to pose for pictures, he produces a makeup sponge from his pocket for a touch-up—'because I've got a lot of face to wipe.'"

Scatman would never attain superstardom, McFarlin concluded: "For one thing, he's interested in—get this—you. Upon being introduced, Scatman beats his interviewer to the punch: 'Where are you from, McFarlin?' 'Have you worked here long?' 'Did you want to be in journalism, or what?'"

In Chicago, Scatman appeared on WLS-TV and WGN-TV.

He also attended a boxing match at Chicago Stadium where Rogers Worthington of *Tempo,* the magazine of the *Chicago Tribune,* watched the crowd's reaction as Scatman made his way toward the popcorn stand:

"Most of his clean-shaven head is covered with a floppy blue toweling hat. But the passing faces of Friday night fight fans split into wide smiles, the mouths start to work, and the name comes out as though they were greeting a long lost friend. . . .

"*'Scatman! Scatman Crothers!'* "

"That recognition continues inside the packed, tense arena, and later in a parking lot where a Warner Bros. limousine awaits. Even when comedian John Belushi walks over and introduces himself, people get happy-eyed and slack mouthed and point: *'Scatman! Heeyy . . . I saw you in Chico and the Man!'*

" 'That's right, baby,' he apes in his limerickese. 'Stick out you can, 'cause heah comes the garbage man.'

"Nobody says anything to Belushi."

Scatman's television work in his seventieth year included guest spots on the series *Project Peacock, Magnum P.I., Dance Fever, Kids Are People, Too, The Posse,* and *Laverne and Shirley.* He worked on the pilot for *The Main Event,* based on the film in which he'd had to turn down a role because of his work in *The Shining.* He appeared in an ABC-TV Movie of the Week called *King of the Hill.* He did a Bicentennial Minute. In fact, he continued to be ubiquitous on television and was still "going strong."

CHAPTER 9

SCAT: MAN

HOLLYWOOD IS IN THE HABIT OF TREATING ITS senior-citizen stars as icons, and Scatman Crothers was no exception. In the early 1980s, he began to receive a number of honors that accrue to Hollywood's elder statesmen, if they have not been offered before.

On April 8, 1981, he was honored by the Hollywood Chamber of Commerce with a sidewalk star on Hollywood's famous "Walk of Fame," directly in front of the Egyptian Theater. Mayor Thomas Bradley of Los Angeles proclaimed that same day "Scatman Crothers Day."

"My PR man, Jerry Zelinka, set all that up, picked the star and the placement of the star right in front of the Egyptian Theater," Scatman recalled. "He saw that I got a good spot. As a matter of fact, he picked my star right between Douglas Fairbanks, Jr., and Cass Dailey.

"I made an acceptance speech. I said, 'I want to thank Mayor Bradley for proclaiming this day Scatman Crothers Day, and also I want to thank the Hollywood Chamber of Commerce and its constituents for bestowing my name on the Hollywood Walk of Fame. I got a whole lot of people to thank, but I think I'll start at home, with my wife, Helen, of forty-four years, who stuck with me through thick and thin—when it got thick, she didn't thin out, she was right there by my side.' "

Helen and Donna were there, as well as James Komack, Jerry Zelinka, Don Schwartz, and other friends and colleagues. Helen recalls that after the ceremonies a group of them had lunch at a long table at a nearby restaurant.

Also in 1981, he had the distinction of serving as grand marshall of the San Fernando Valley Fair. "I keep meaning to ask my PR man what I'm supposed to do—arrest people or what?" Scatman quipped.

His hand and footprints were encased in wax for permanent display at the Movieland Wax Museum.

In 1982, Don Schwartz decided to celebrate Scatman's fifty years in show business, choosing as his starting date the year 1932 when Scatman first called himself the Scat Man. If anyone had thought of it, a similar celebration could have been held back in 1974, for Scatman was fourteen when he first started playing in the Terre Haute speakeasies. But in 1974, Scatman was just getting started on *Chico,* and neither he nor Schwartz had the leisure to mark anniversaries.

"It was held at the Little Club in Beverly Hills where Joan Rivers used to perform," says Steve Tisherman. "It was quite a night. Helen and Donna were there, and some of Scat's close friends and business associates. Jimmy Komack, producer of *Chico,* was there. People got up impromptu and performed or paid tribute. I remember that Redd Foxx did comedy. He and Scat got up together and did some routines. Scat played his banjo, of course; he was an orchestra unto himself." Helen remembers that Jane Russell was another star who honored Scat that night.

One of the things Redd Foxx did was to present Scatman

with an "Oscar" for Best Supporting Actor Left on the Cutting-Room Floor for what nobody saw him do in *One Flew Over the Cuckoo's Nest.*

In September 1983, Scatman was the first recipient of the Russian River Jazz Festival's Lifetime Achievement Award at a three-day event in Guerneville, California. Dave Brubeck and Stan Getz, who had wanted to go with Scatman to Pocatello, Idaho, forty years earlier, participated in the salute.

In 1984, he was the subject of one of Ralph Edwards's *This Is Your Life* programs, hosted by Joseph Campanella. All preparations for the show were made in secret. Terre Haute Mayor Pete Chalos, John Wesley Lyda, and Demetrius Ewing were flown out to Los Angeles from Terre Haute with the understanding that they were to tell no one but their immediate families the purpose of their trip. Helen, Donna, and Phil Harris, who made the trip to Los Angeles from his new home in Rancho Mirage, in Palm Desert, California, were also sworn to secrecy. Scatman was led to believe that he was simply going to have a night on the town when he was taken to the Voyageur nightclub in Los Angeles.

When he realized that he was on *This Is Your Life,* Scatman broke down briefly, blowing his nose into a big white handkerchief a couple of times before he regained his composure. But he recognized the voices of Pete Chalos, to whom he spoke in Greek, Lyda, and Ewing. By the time he and Phil Harris did a duet of "Chattanooga Shoeshine Boy," he was having the time of his life.

The show was not ordinarily seen in Terre Haute, but because of Scatman's appearance a local TV station arranged to air the segment. Scatman's hometown had wholeheartedly, if somewhat belatedly, begun to celebrate him, too.

Scatman accepted these honors with great humility, basking in the limelight. But he had no intention of simply sitting back and resting on his achievements. He was still working.

In 1981 he appeared in the pilot for a series for NBC titled *Revenge of the Gray Gang,* a comedy-drama about five retired senior citizens who band together to battle crime. Scatman played Reuben Milo, a retired electrician. Unfortunately, the proposed series got no farther than the pilot.

He then signed to co-star with Mickey Rooney in a new half-hour TV sitcom titled *One of the Boys* for NBC. Rooney played Oliver Nugent, a retired sixty-six-year-old grandfather who moves in with his grandson and his grandson's college roommate. Scatman played the role of Bernard Solomon, Oliver's friend. The series was a mid-season entry that ran for a total of nine episodes between January and June 1982 and then made a brief reappearance for three episodes in August of the same year. Ratings were disappointing, however, and NBC did not renew the show for the fall.

Next, Scatman signed on as a regular in a new, sixty-minute dramatic series for NBC called *Casablanca,* starring David Soul of *Starsky and Hutch* fame. Based on the 1942 film of the same name starring Humphrey Bogart and Ingrid Bergman, the TV series was set in 1941 in Nazi-occupied French Morocco and followed the adventures of Rick Blaine, the owner of Rick's Café Americain, as he involved himself in the plight of people needing help. Scatman played Sam, the piano player, the role that had been played by Dooley Wilson in the original film. "He had to fake it," says Helen. "He didn't know how to play the piano."

First aired in April 1983, this show, which was produced by David Wolper, who had been executive producer for *Roots,* was also a mid-season entry. Pulled off the air for further tinkering after only a few episodes, it briefly reappeared in August, but it, too, was not renewed.

"I'll be honest with you, it was a little disappointing when they canceled the series," Scatman told Robert Greenberger of *Starlog* in 1983. "They never really gave 'Casablanca' a chance. David Soul did a great job portraying Rick. Humphrey Bogart was no comparison to what David did. David was sexier, more exciting, more everything. You needed the right time, promotion and everything else that goes into making a show a success. If the thing's not promoted and not put on at the right time, I don't care what it is, it won't go. Whenever I travel around the country, people tell me they loved 'Casablanca.' "

Scatman, however, got plenty of work in television as a guest star in other series, including *Benson, It Takes Two, Dance Fever,* and *Hee Haw.* He also appeared in an ABC-TV Movie of the Week titled *Where Are My Children?* a special called *Inside America* with Jack Nicholson, and "Working," a *Playhouse 90* presentation.

In the early 1980s, he appeared on *The Fantasy Show,* short-lived but national. Stars brought on their protégés to perform. Invited to bring on his protégé, Scatman chose Clora Bryant, the female trumpet player.

"I never knew he thought of me as his protégé until we did the show," says Bryant, who had to have been one of the most veteran "protégés" ever to appear on *The Fantasy Show.* "But we had gotten back together for his revue, and over the years, anytime he could, he would throw gigs my way, so I guess he thought of me. He did a couple songs; one of them was 'Still Going Strong.' Then he brought me on, and we did a number together. It was fun, and I really appreciated his spreading the word and putting my name out there, because it's very hard for a female horn player. The competition is so stiff with the men, and a lot of men don't even want to hear it. After I did that TV show, I got quite a few calls from back East, because it was a national show. In fact, Dizzy called me. And the guy from the Parisian Room called me."

Scatman often wrote songs for his friends. Clora Bryant wrote poems for hers. "I've got a stack of them," she says. "I wrote one for Louis [Armstrong, of whom she did a great imitation], Dexter Gordon, Sammy Davis, Jr., Sarah Vaughan. I trace their lives in verse poems; that's the way I honor them. The one I wrote for Scat is called 'Portrait of Scat.'" Seventeen verses long, the poem ends with these lines:

I can still see Scatman with the garbage can
In the role he played on "Chico and the Man"
Oh! How he could light up that old boob tube every
   week
He had a way about him

You knew you couldn't doubt him
Cause he had a flair for comedy and plain ole "tongue
   in the cheek."

In 1981, Scatman filmed *Deadly Eyes* (aka *The Rats*), a low-budget movie released in 1982 in Europe and in 1984 in the United States by Northshore Investments/Golden Communications. Sam Groom starred in this throwback to the science-fiction dramas of the 1950s about a special breed of rats growing to unusually large proportions and terrorizing a city. Scatman played George Foskins. "These rats eat me up and kill me," he said, adding in his characteristic limerickese, "First, it was the ax, then, it was the rats. What's next? maybe a vampire—the bats."

The following year, he played Early in *Two of a Kind*, starring John Travolta and Olivia Newton-John, a 20th Century–Fox Christmas 1982 release about two down-on-their-luck types who are given a week to prove their worth to the angels. Representatives of both good and evil spend the time trying to convert the couple. Oliver Reed plays the Devil. Charles Durning and Scatman play angels.

"I'm an angel—typecasting," Scatman laughed. "First of all, I'm a New York bus driver who loves to play golf. I'm somewhat arrogant, but by the end I get serious. I try to get everyone together as a team because then we'll all be happy. The film mostly has to do with love." Unfortunately, it was not loved by audiences, and bombed at the box office.

He also played Dexter Jones, a high school coach with a fondness for liquor, in *Zapped!*, starring Scott Baio and Heather Thomas, an Apple-Rose production released by Embassy.

The number of films in which Scatman appeared in the course of his career would make a great trivia question. Not even the keenest movie buff could remember all the small parts he played in relatively forgettable films. What movie goers remember are the big roles in major films, and Scatman had one more of those to add to his list in *Twilight Zone: The Movie.*

The film was planned as an homage to the Rod Serling TV series *Twilight Zone,* by four young directors, John Landis, Steven

Spielberg, Joe Dante, and the Autralian George Miller. The first segment, directed by Landis, will be remembered best for the tragedy that took place during filming, when a helicopter crashed, killing star Vic Morrow and two Vietnamese-American children.

Spielberg's segment was the second. Scatman starred as Mr. Bloom, a new arrival at the Sunnyvale Rest Home who shows a group of fellow residents how to recapture the freedom and wonder of childhood by playing the game Kick the Can.

The part could well have been written especially for Scatman, whose zest for life remained undiminished, who had decided, "I'd rather be my own age, and keep a fresh, young mind," and who was known to aver, "This old man still has a little magic left in him."

"I loved Mr. Bloom," said Scatman. "At the wrap party, I met George Clayton Johnson [who wrote the original episode and collaborated on the new version]. He said, 'Scat, I was hoping they would get you for this part.' "

He and Spielberg enjoyed working together. Spielberg took Scatman to meet his mother. "She had this Milky Way restaurant over on Pico and Doheney," Scatman recalled. "She was a charming lady. She said he was born in Phoenix. I didn't know he was born in Phoenix."

Spielberg said to Scatman, "You've written a song for Stanley [Kubrick], for Clint Eastwood. I've never had anyone write a song for me." So Scatman obliged with "A Remarkable Young Man." "He was just like a little kid [when I sang his song for him]," said Scatman. "He was so happy."

On the set of *Twilight Zone: The Movie*, Spielberg went up to Scatman one day and said, "I have a new name for you, Scatman. You're the black E.T." Scatman took it as a compliment, but said later, "Now I must go see *E.T.*—so I know what that means."

The film was released in 1983, and while the Spielberg segment itself was criticized as coy and slick, Scatman won considerable praise for his portrayal of the hero, although Richard Combs in *The Monthly Film Bulletin* wrote that the segment was "a

fairy-tale with a message . . . treated with such whimsical over-
load that Scatman Crothers becomes an Uncle-Tomish genie in
a more insidious, and punishable, instance of racism than anything indicated in the first [Landis] segment."

Around 1984, Scatman decided it was time to slow down.
Partly, his decision was due to his age, for strenuous work now
tired him. But partly, too, it was because Helen had decided they
should no longer travel together. "We'd been all over the place,"
says Helen. "I went to Australia with him. We went to all the
celebrity golf tournaments. Nothing ever happened to make me
afraid. Then, around 1984, we were on a plane together. We
were going to Las Vegas to do a TV special with Jonathan Winters. There was a terrible storm. It was thundering and light-
ning, and it threw my coffee cup against the wall. I prayed, 'God,
just let us get off this plane.' We landed safely, but after that I
decided we were never flying together again. I didn't want something to happen to us and have Donna left alone."

Moreover, Scatman did not want to work as much because
Helen was not feeling well. "He would do the shopping for
me—he was a better shopper than I was," says Helen. "He would
cook for me, feed me. If I was in pain, he would say, 'Honey, I
wish I could take that pain from you. I wish God would take that
pain from you and give it to me."

Said Donna in 1986, "The love between my parents is just
amazing. I don't remember his ever leaving the house without
kissing her. I remember when he was on *The Paper Chase* [1985].
We went to the wrap party. He got up and started singing, and
all of a sudden the tears were just streaming all down his face.
I'm thinking, what is wrong with him? Everybody was looking at
me and looking at him and wondering, why is he crying? Later,
he said to me, 'When I saw you looking up at me, I saw Mother.
I saw Mommy all in your eyes.' "

Not wanting to leave Helen was one reason why Scatman
turned down a solid offer to appear on Broadway, according to
Don Schwartz: "He was offered a part opposite Jason Robards,
Jr., in a very difficult play called *I'm Not Rappaport*. I very badly
wanted him to do it, because that show would have brought him

to stardom, the real big thing. He needed that one thing to go over the edge, because you can go along playing good, even great, scenes with John Wayne and Jack Nicholson, but you need your own vehicle. The producer came out and read with him, tried to talk him into it.

"He didn't want to be parted from his wife. I also think he was a little hesitant about learning that many lines. I'm not sure about that, but I think when you get to be seventy-two years old, you don't have the same spirit of adventure as a younger man. I fought with him over that. He'd say, 'Why do I need Broadway?' I'd say, 'Almost everybody has been made bigger by going to Broadway.' He'd say, 'You're right. I guess So-and-so came from Broadway, and So-and-so came from Broadway.' But then he'd say again, 'Why do I need Broadway?' Anyway, the producer could see that he didn't really want to do it, and that was that.

"One day I got into the elevator in my building and Jason Robards got on with me. I told him I was Scatman's agent, and he said he'd wanted to do *I'm Not Rappaport* with him very badly. In fact, the reason he didn't do it was because Scatman wouldn't and they couldn't get anyone comparable to him. He thought that Scatman was just the talent for that type of role."

I'm Not Rappaport, which first played off-Broadway at the American Place Theatre before moving to the Street of Dreams in 1985, starred Judd Hirsch and Cleavon Little. Don Schwartz's dream of seeing Scatman on Broadway went unfulfilled.

Scatman continued to do voice-overs. Says Steve Tisherman, who left the Schwartz agency and formed his own agency in 1983, "He loved voice-overs. It was simple work, the time-span was not vast, and it was fun for him to be himself and be on in front of a mike with a character. He would have done that until the day he dropped. It was the perfect vehicle for him."

Fortunately, such a vehicle came along in *The Transformers,* an animated three-part series that focused on the battle between the inhabitants of a long-ago mechanical planet called Cybertron. All the inhabitants could transform themselves into other things, and the main plot was a battle between the Autobots, the good guys, and the Decepticons, the bad guys. The show lasted three years, from 1985 to 1988.

The Transformers were toys," says Tisherman. "They were robots, and you could change their shape into tanks or airplanes by just bending the head and pushing it under. Thus the name 'Transformers.' Those toys were very big in the late seventies and early eighties, and the cartoon show was a spin-off. It was a syndicated TV show produced by Sunbow in association with Marvel, which produced the toys. They must have done about one hundred and fifty episodes, and there were a lot of characters in the show—it was probably the biggest cast I ever saw. Several clients of mine were in it—Mark Jordan, Joe Leahy, Peter Cullen, in addition to Scatman—and every few months, or cycle period, they would cast for new characters. Scatman was in about fifty of the shows, and Helen is still collecting residuals."

Scatman also continued to accept television guest spots that involved just working a week here and there, appearing on *Matt Houston, The Love Boat,* the short-lived *Pryor's Place, Hotel,* and other series. He appeared in a special called *Juvenile Jury* and went to Las Vegas to appear in *The Wonderful World of Jonathan Winters.*

But for a lifelong workaholic like Scatman, the middle eighties were a time of comparative leisure, when he was more likely to leave the house to play golf than to work. He kept active. When he didn't play golf, he rode his bicycle, and he swam every chance he got. He often spent time with Donna, with whom he had become much closer in his later years. They would go to dinner and to clubs together. Still, he was home a lot.

Helen was not accustomed to his being home so much, and it suddenly occurred to her that they lived in a very large house. "There's a hall this way, and a hall that way," she says, "and I wasn't always sure where he was. So I bought two whistles. I gave him a whistle, and I had a whistle, and I told him, when you want me, whistle. He whistled all right, three o'clock in the morning, three o'clock in the afternoon. I'd be in the kitchen doing something, and I'd think I heard him whistling, and I'd go to him and there he'd be just snoring. But I didn't mind."

Scatman did accept a role in the 1985 film *Journey of Natty Gann* as a Depression-era street vendor named Shuman who befriends the spunky fourteen-year-old Natty (Meredith Salenger) as she starts on her journey across the country to find her father. But except for that work, all he did in 1985 was a segment on *The Paper Chase* and a PBS special with Ossie Davis and Ruby Dee called *In Other Words*.

He did, however, continue to do a great deal of charity work. He participated in several celebrity golf tournaments, among them the Roy Clark Classic to benefit the Tulsa, Oklahoma, Children's Medical Center. He did more telethons. He went frequently to the Actors' Home, as he had been doing for many years, to entertain the retired show-business people who lived there. In spite of all his TV and film work, he still considered himself "the Scat Man," singer and entertainer.

The same year *The Journey of Natty Gann* was released, Scatman learned he had cancer. According to Helen, for some months he had been spitting up blood. He'd gone to his doctor, but X rays had shown nothing. The doctor suggested that he might have a bleeding ulcer that didn't show up; or perhaps when he coughed, he strained himself and broke blood vessels. But Helen felt it was more than that.

"He had to go to Washington, D.C., to film a special with Ossie Davis and Ruby Dee," she recalls. "It was being done at Howard University Hospital, so I told him when he got to the hospital to see one of the doctors there. I don't know the name of the doctor he saw there, but whoever it was told him that when he got home he should have a CT scan done on his chest. So on July 10, as soon as he got back, we went and had a CT scan done, and they found out that he had lung cancer—a tumor on one of his lungs.

"The doctor came into Scat's hospital room where Donna and I were sitting. He sat down on the edge of the bed and said, 'I have some sad news to tell you.' When he said Scat had cancer, I put my fist in my mouth. I said I couldn't believe it, it couldn't be true. He said, 'It is, Mrs. Crothers, but don't worry about it. He's a strong man, he's got a strong constitution. He's gonna pull out of this."

"They operated, but once they got inside, they found out that the tumor was pressing up against the main artery to his heart. They couldn't do anything, so they just sewed him back up. Then they started him on radiation."

Cards, telegrams, and calls came from all across the country. President Ronald Reagan, who had himself recently undergone surgery for removal of a cancerous growth on his nose, wrote a get-well letter, addressing it "From one recuperator to another, get well soon," and wishing Scatman "as speedy a recovery as I am experiencing. We both have bookings to keep and I know that you are anxious to get back on the golf course just as I can't wait to get on horseback."

Scatman had radiation treatments for seven weeks. During that time, he was weak, but he did not feel especially ill. He even played golf occasionally, although he tired easily and usually did not finish a game. Teddy Edwards was still a frequent golfing partner. "He had to give up smoking weed when he got sick," says Edwards. "He loved to smoke that weed. When he found out he was sick, he called me and he took me by his house and gave me his jar of weed. He said, 'Man, I can't smoke it anymore. You take it.' He have me a whole big box of bamboo cigarette paper."

"He put on weight," Helen recalls. "He'd never weighed over one hundred sixty-three or one hundred sixty-five, but he was lying around a lot and eating. We were both eating breakfast, lunch, and dinner, and snacking in between. He got up to about a hundred-eighty, and I put on about ten pounds. Later, we had to go on a diet."

On November 2, 1985, Scatman participated via telephone hookup in ceremonies honoring him at the state convention of the Indiana chapter of the NAACP. He was supposed to have been the guest of honor at the convention, which was held in Terre Haute. Mayor Pete Chalos had ordered a plaque for him and had designated that Saturday as Scatman Crothers Day.

The alumni association of Indiana State University had elected him an honorary alumnus and also prepared a plaque. "Keep track of them and don't lose them," said John Wesley Lyda, president of the local NAACP, of the pile of plaques.

Scatman, who had not been back to Terre Haute since a 1969 visit to his family, was deeply moved and regretted not having been able to attend. But the weeks of radiation therapy had left him too weak to travel. His spirit was still strong, however. "I love you," he told the assembled crowd over the Hulman Center's loudspeaker.

Three weeks later, on November 22, he wrote a letter to the author concerning the proposal for his autobiography: "I saw my radiation Dr. on October 23rd, they took Xrays, and the Dr. said, 'Mr. Crothers, I'll see you in six months.' Isn't that a blessing? So evidently I'm in remission."

Scatman felt well enough both physically and mentally to accept a role in a new series for television titled *Morningstar/Eveningstar*. Obviously a vehicle for Scatman, the CBS series was also clearly inspired by the segment in *Twilight Zone: The Movie* in which he had starred. It centered around the lives of a number of elderly people who lived together in a large house and starred Sylvia Sidney, among others. Scatman played the part of Excell Dennis, an elderly actor working as a lounge pianist.

It is customary for a proposed star in a TV series or film to undergo a physical examination before being signed to a role. Scatman having been diagnosed as suffering from cancer the previous year, the producers required that he be examined by two doctors. Both pronounced him fit, his cancer in remission.

At first, Scatman wasn't sure he wanted to do another series, but he had waited more than ten years for one he could call his own. He read the script and thought it was funny. He told himself it was only a half-hour show and wouldn't be as difficult as an hour-long show, as *Casablanca* had been. Moreover, the money was right. So he signed on.

Helen had mixed feelings about his being in a new series. "I'm glad because he's in *TV Guide* and in *Jet* and all," she said in early 1986. "But in a way I'm sorry, because the hours are so long, and he gets so tired and he's not used to that. He hasn't done a weekly series for a while."

The schedule did prove to be too grueling. Don Schwartz remembered that Scatman was uncharacteristically crabby on the set. "He wasn't comfortable in his dressing room," says Schwartz. "He was used to Winnebagos, and he just couldn't handle that dressing room. He asked for a lot of attention, but I think he was sicker than he realized then." On one occasion, he was hospitalized at Beverly Hills Medical Center for three days after complaining of flulike symptoms.

"He said his stomach was hurting," says Helen, "and I called the doctor, and the doctor told me to rush him over to Beverly Hills Medical Center. This was on a Sunday. On Tuesday, someone from UPI called his agent and said, 'We heard Scatman Crothers passed away.' They said, 'No way, he's got a little flu, that's all.'"

But the rumor was out. Friends called Helen to say they'd heard Scatman had died. The *National Enquirer* called Don Schwartz to confirm it. Helen remembers that a black radio station announced his death, and she was determined to sue. But she was far more concerned with caring for her husband, and he was not of a mind to bring suit against anyone.

In June 1986, Scatman left the cast of *Morningstar/Eveningstar,* citing ill health and explaining that the series was too much for him. "I just want to do a few pictures a year and maybe a few guest shots," he said.

Helen recalls, "He said, 'Honey, I am going to start cutting down on all of these things. We have to spend more time together. I think he had a premonition that he might not be around too long. He got tired easily. We went to the Charley Pride Golf Tournament in Santa Fe, and they always have a big barbecue afterward, but he didn't feel like going to it, so we left early. Same thing with the Bob Hope Classic. We left early. He had to stop doing the Arthritis Telethons—he'd been one of the first to do them."

Scatman could not even finish a round of golf. He complained of pain in his chest again. Soon he was back in the hospital. Helen moved to the hospital with him, as she had during his earlier stay. "They put a bed in his room for me. He wouldn't take a pill unless I said it was all right," she says.

Scatman was put on chemotherapy. He couldn't eat and was fed intravenously, but he was in good spirits. "He asked the nurse to have me bring him his guitar," says Helen, and she brought him the same trusty instrument that he had been playing since 1931. Scat said it still played well, so he had never replaced it. "He and the nurse would sing together. He was really sick, but the two of them would sing away. There was another little nurse. Every time she came by, she'd say, 'Mr. Crothers, where's that big, beautiful smile?' His face would just light up.

"Donna dressed up special for him every time she visited the hospital. So many people called and sent get-well wishes and plants. We had over two-hundred-fifty plants and vases of flowers from every studio—Disney, Warner Bros., you name it. And all the stars he'd ever worked with—Lee Majors, Clint Eastwood, Eileen Brennan, Mickey Rooney. A lot of the stars wanted to visit him, but he'd had a couple of visitors, and everyone could see that he was too tired. Casey Kasem's wife, Jean, came by with a huge bouquet of balloons, and I let her come up, and she stayed a little while. Phil Harris came. But after a while, we decided against having visitors."

They still accepted calls. Says Phil Harris, "I saw him when he was sick, when he went to the hospital, and then when he got out, I called him almost every day. He thought he was going to beat it, but it was in his throat."

Helen recalls, "One night Scat grabbed his throat. I rang for the nurse to increase the dosage on his morphine drip, and then I went out to find the doctor. I wanted a CT scan of his throat, his chest, his stomach, his brain, everything. So they took the scans, and the next evening when the doctor came in, I could tell by his face that there was something wrong. Scat was still thinking he was going to be all right. He said, 'Doctor, you gonna have me back on the golf course?' The doctor said yes because he didn't want him to know how bad it was. The cancer had spread up to his esophagus, which was why his throat was hurting. I said, 'How long?' and the doctor said two-and-a-half, three months. He hit it right on the nose."

With the help of nurses, Helen cared for Scatman at home, where he was surrounded by familiar things. She tried to make their lives seem as normal as possible and made sure she was always cheerful.

But it was difficult for Helen to be upbeat as the weeks passed and she could see her husband's condition worsen. "His mind was going," she says. "Jerry [Zelinka, Scatman's publicist] came to see him. He said, 'Hi, Scat,' and Scat just stared at him. Jerry had tears in his eyes. Then a few moments later, Scat looked up and said, 'Hi, Jerry, old buddy!' Scat would slip in and out.

"A lot of people wanted to come and visit him, but his doctor didn't think that was a good idea."

Helen worried that having no visitors would depress her husband. "Scat knew," she says. "At first he had a really good frame of mind. But in the last three months or so, he didn't laugh as much. He used to love ball games, but he didn't want to watch any sports. He didn't have much to say at all. He'd shake his head yes or no. The last week he couldn't talk at all. We'd hug and kiss and hug and kiss every day. I'd tell him how much I loved him and how much our daughter loved him, and he'd just squeeze my hand. He suffered a lot."

Scatman died on November 22, 1986, exactly one year after he wrote that hopeful letter to the author.

After he had realized that he was not going to recover, Scatman and Helen had discussed his funeral. She'd asked, "Honey, would you like a private funeral?" And he'd answered, "No, honey. My public made me, and if they want to come to my funeral, I want them there." So the funeral that was held the following Tuesday, November 25, at Forest Lawn Memorial Park, was a public one. About three hundred mourners gathered at the Old North Church to hear Scatman eulogized.

James Komack, producer of *Chico and the Man*, delivered the eulogy. "He never treated himself as if he was a star," said

Komack. "What you saw on the screen was what you got at home. He considered his job to be making people happy. He did his job well."

Jack Nicholson recalled, "He had this saying: 'May you never die because I'm going to live forever.' He started today with his wish."

Later, recalled Don Schwartz, "Jack said to me, 'I love Scat. I think he was a much more consummate actor than anybody ever realized.' "

After the funeral was over, the full realization of her loss dawned on Helen. "I don't know what I would have done without Donna after Scat died," she says. She made halfhearted attempts to go through Scatman's belongings and sort through papers, but she had no intention of getting rid of his things.

"We were together forty-nine years," she says. "We were like one person."

One day a package arrived in the mail, and when Helen opened it, she found the long-lost scrapbook that she had kept for Scat during the first years of their marriage. While they were in Akron, Ohio, in 1945, a man had borrowed it and not returned it.

"I guess this man had an attack of conscience," says Helen, "because he finally sent it back after forty-something years. I remember that when I opened the cover, the pages just crumbled."

The scrapbook brought back happy memories, and Helen occasionally turns its dry and yellowed pages. She also listens to tapes of radio shows that Scatman did over the years. "I miss him so much," she says. "I feel as if half of me went with him."

Helen had not been feeling well herself while her husband was in the final months of his life, but she had put off having a checkup in order to take care of him. Two months after she buried Scatman, she learned that she, too, had cancer and underwent surgery. She was recuperating when representatives of the Black Filmmakers Hall of Fame contacted her about inducting Scatman posthumously.

"They'd been trying to get him for years," she says, "but he was always working or something, and just hadn't been able to fit it into his schedule. So when they called me, I knew he would want me to go in his place. It was February 1987, just a month after my operation. Donna went with me.

"The streets were just lined with people. They had to block off the area where the limo stopped. There were all sorts of stars there—Clifton Davis and his wife, Sammy Davis, Jr. When it came time to present the award to Scat, they talked about all the things he did, and said what a great asset he was to the black community and how everybody respected him. Then they showed a clip from *The Shining,* and then they brought me up onstage to accept the award.

"I said, 'First of all, I want you to know that my husband and I were married forty-nine years,' and then the house came down. And then I said if Scat had been there to accept the award, he would have thanked the black filmmakers for inducting him into their Hall of Fame because it was a great honor. And I said, then he would thank all you beautiful people for being here because he loved everybody. And that's all I could say, because I started crying. I don't know what I was thinking about. I should have taken Donna up on that stage with me."

True to his word, Scatman had provided well for Helen and Donna. "We have all the money we need," says Helen.

Thanks to the miracle of television, Scatman is often seen in homes across the nation on reruns of *Laverne and Shirley, The Love Boat,* and the like. His voice is also heard in reruns of the various cartoon shows on which he worked. In addition to keeping his memory alive, these reruns of his shows continue to earn money for Helen. "I still get residuals checks," she says. "I remember one day I got twelve separate checks for residuals from *The Transformers.*"

Says Steve Tisherman, "*The Transformers* is in syndication in both the domestic and foreign markets. The payment is about eighteen dollars an episode, but when you were in fifty of the shows, as Scatman was, it adds up. Helen asked about my commission, but I told her to forget the commission."

Scatman also continues, in death, to give to charity. "Scat

gave to one charity that distributes the contributions to other charities," says Helen. "Every check I get today, there is something taken out of it."

Unfortunately, *Chico and the Man* has never gone into syndication domestically, thus depriving new generations of Americans of the chance to enjoy Scatman.

Helen Crothers says, "It was such a great show, and they had whites, blacks, Hispanics, in it. I called Jimmy Komack to find out why it wasn't in reruns, and he said, 'I think it's because of the way Freddie died.' "

Recently, *Chico and the Man* has been syndicated in Europe, and Helen has been receiving residuals.

The Shining is aired on television with some frequency, and on rare occasions one can see Scatman in one of his old movies, or in a syndicated TV drama.

For the Black History Month observance in February 1988, Pacific Bell contacted Helen for permission to use his photograph in a monthlong tribute to several late black stars, among them Dorothy Dandridge, Mahalia Jackson, and Jesse Owens, called *Legends Among Us*. Helen gave her permission and was pleased to receive a number of telephone calls from friends who saw the Pacific Bell spots on television.

Even four years after Scatman's death, Helen still gets invitations for him to appear. "The other day he was invited to be in a Christmas parade," she said in the fall of 1990. "I just wrote back and told them he couldn't make it."

Helen would like to see Scatman's songs recorded. "He always wanted to have them recorded by someone big, like Billy Eckstine," she says. "I have them all together, and I mean to do something about getting them put on an album."

They're little ditties, many about Helen and love, many comic, like "The Biscuit Song." On paper, they don't always rhyme and they often seem corny, but when Scatman sang them with his big smile and his perfect sense of timing, they worked. One hopes that, if Helen gets her wish, whoever does record them will study Scatman's style so he can do justice to them.

Even so, they won't be the same without Scatman to sing them. He was a unique man and a unique personality, possessed of a heart and a cheery outlook on life that can never be duplicated. A good man who devoted his life to making other people happy, he reaped the rewards in happiness of his own.

APPENDIX

SCATMAN'S FILMS AND TELEVISION APPEARANCES

MOTION PICTURES

Yes, Sir, Mr. Bones (1951, Lippert Pictures)
Meet Me at the Fair (1952, Universal)
Return of Gilbert and Sullivan (1952)
East of Sumatra (1953, Universal)
Walking My Baby Back Home (1953, Universal)
Johnny Dark (1954, Universal)
Between Heaven and Hell (1956, 20th Century–Fox)
The Nat King Cole Story (1956, Universal)
The Gift of Love (1958, 20th Century–Fox)
The Sins of Rachel Cade (1960, Warner Bros.)
The Patsy (1964, Paramount)
Lady in a Cage (1964, Paramount)
The Family Jewels (1965, Paramount)
Three on a Couch (1966, Columbia)
Hello, Dolly! (1969, 20th Century–Fox)

The Aristocats (1970, Disney Animation)
The Great White Hope (1970, 20th Century–Fox)
Bloody Mama (1970, American International)
Chandler (1971, MGM; originally titled *Open Shadow*)
The King of Marvin Gardens (1972, Paramount)
Lady Sings the Blues (1972, Motown/Paramount)
Another Day at the Races (1972)
Detroit 9000 (1973, General)
Slaughter's Big Rip-Off (1973, American International)
Black Belt Jones (1974, Warner Bros.)
Linda Lovelace for President (1974)
Truck Turner (1974, American International)
Whiffs (1975, 20th Century–Fox)
The Fortune (1975, Columbia)
One Flew Over the Cuckoo's Nest (1975, United Artists)
Coonskin (1975, A.F. Bryanston)
Friday Foster (1975, American International)
Stay Hungry (1976, United Artists)
The Shootist (1976, Paramount)
Silver Streak (1977, 20th Century–Fox)
Mean Dog Blues (1978, American International)
The Cheap Detective (1978, Columbia)
That's Life (1979, unreleased)
Scavenger Hunt (1979, 20th Century–Fox)
Bronco Billy (1980, Warner Bros.)
The Shining (1980, Warner Bros.)
The Rats (1982, Northshore Investments/Golden Communications; also as *Deadly Eyes*, 1983, Warner Bros.)
Zapped! (1982, Embassy; orginally titled *The Wiz Kid*)
Two of a Kind (1983, 20th Century–Fox; orginally titled *Second Chance*)
Twilight Zone: The Movie (1983, Warner Bros.)
The Journey of Natty Gann (1984, Disney)

TELEVISION

Cartoon Voices

Time for Beany 1950
Beany and Cecil 1950s
Hong Kong Phooey 1974–76, 1978, 1979, 1981
The Harlem Globetrotters 1970–73, 1978
Scooby's All-Star Laff-A-Lympics 1977–78
Super Globetrotters 1977–79
The Skatebirds 1977
The Paw Paws 1985
The Transformers 1985–86

Miniseries and Movies

Mary Ann 1975
Man on the Outside 1975
Christy Anderson, USN 1976
Roots 1977
Undercover Elephant 1977
King of the Hill 1980
Working 1981
National Lampoon Goes to the Movies 1981
Missing Children: A Mother's Story

Specials

Disney on Parade 1972
Moments with Dora 1973
The Sty of the Blind Pig 1974
Jonathan Winters Presents 200 Years of American Humor 1976
Banjo the Woodpile Cat 1976
Joys 1976

Dean Martin Roast for Ted Knight 1977
The Harlem Globetrotters 1978
Weekend of Foul Play with John Ritter 1978
NBC 25-Year Salute to "Wonderful World of Disney" 1978
Comedy Shop 1978
The Bob Hope Special 1978
Puppy's Great Adventures 1978
Opening Night 1978
Sunshine on the Way 1980
Bicentennial Minutes 1980
The Harlem Globetrotters on Gilligan's Island (extension episode) 1981
Inside America, with Jack Nicholson 1982
Wonderful World of Jonathan Winters in Las Vegas 1984
Juvenile Jury 1984
Pat Boone, USA, Christmas Special 1984
Ossie and Ruby . . . In Other Words 1985

Series Guest Appearances

Beulah 1950–52
Alfred Hitchcock Presents ("Don't Interrupt") 1958
Bourbon Street Beat ("The Mourning Clock") 1959
Dragnet ("The Big High") 1967
Love American Style ("Love and the Dummies") 1970
Barefoot in the Park ("Something Fishy") 1970
Governor and J.J. 1970
Bewitched ("Three Men and a Witch on a Horse") 1971
The Good Life ("Butterfield ATE 3526") 1971
Nichols ("Eddie Joe") 1971
Love American Style ("Somethin' Fishy") 1972
Adam 12 1972
Farraday and Company ("The Riddle of Smokey Stover") 1973
Griff ("Isolate and Destroy") 1973
Ironside ("The Last Payment") 1973
Kojak ("The Corrupter") 1973

Temperatures Rising ("The Mothers") 1973
McMillan and Wife ("Downshift to Danger") 1974
Love American Style ("Love and the Perfect Wedding") 1974
Dora's New World 1974
Toma ("The Street") 1974
Mannix ("The Green Man") 1974
The Odd Couple ("The Subway Show") 1974
The Night Stalker ("The Zombie") 1974
Sanford and Son ("The Stand-in") 1974
Petrocelli ("Jubilee Jones") 1975
Celebrity Sweepstakes 1976
Lohman and Harkley 1976
Starsky and Hutch ("Long Walk on a Short Dirt Road") 1977
The Gong Show 1977
The Love Boat ("Isaac's History Lesson") 1978
Charlie's Angels ("Angels in Vegas") 1978
Flying High ("The Marcy Connection") 1978
Welcome Back, Kotter 1978
Vegas ("The Usurper") 1979
The Incredible Hulk ("The Magician") 1979
Make Me Laugh 1979
Laverne and Shirley 1980
Project Peacock ("Grandpa Will You Run with Me?") 1980
Kids Are People Too 1980
Magnum, P.I. ("Lest We Forget") 1980
Special Treat ("Sunshine's on the Way") 1980
The Posse 1981
Benson ("In the Red") 1982
It Takes Two ("Death Penalty") 1982
Taxi ("A Grand Gesture") 1983
Hotel ("Confrontations") 1983
Hill Street Blues ("Parting Is Such Sweet Sorrow") 1984
Love Boat ("The Christ") 1984
Pryor's Place ("Too Old Too Soon Too Smart Too Late") 1984
Matt Houston ("Death Trap") 1984
We Got it Made ("Mickey Makes the Grade") 1984
The Love Boat ("Santa, Santa, Santa") 1984

Matt Houston ("Death Trap") 1985
The Paper Chase 1985

Series Pilots

Big Daddy 1973
Vegas 1978
The Main Event 1980
Revenge of the Gray Gang 1981
We've Got it Made 1984

Series Starring Roles

Chico and the Man 1974–1977
One of the Boys 1982
Casablanca 1983
Morningstar/Eveningstar 1986

Talk-Show Appearances

The Tonight Show (10 times) 1975
The Mike Douglas Show 1975
The Dinah Shore Show (2 times) 1975
The Mike Douglas Show (2 times) 1976
Sammy and Company 1976
The Dinah Shore Show 1976
The Tonight Show (2 times) 1976
The David Steinberg Show 1976
Dinah! (2 times) 1977
The Tonight Show (3 times) 1977
Dinah! 1978
The Tonight Show 1978
The Tonight Show 1979
The Tonight Show 1982

Variety Shows

Dixie Showboat 1948–1950
Colgate Comedy Hour 1951–1954
The Rich Little Show 1976
The Jim Nabors Show 1978
Dance Fever 1980
Dance Fever 1981
Ad Lib 1981
The John Davidson Show 1981
Hee Haw 1982
America's Music 1983

INDEX

215